INSPECT & PROTECT

A Protocol for Avoiding Lawsuits and Disputes

A NOTE ON THE TEXT

This book includes some articles that were published elsewhere many years ago, so the references to time and tense throughout are not necessarily uniform. Regardless, this book is dedicated to those inspectors who've been victimized by frivolous lawsuits and a legal system that has not only made a mockery of justice but appears at times to have forsaken the very principles on which it rests.

I'm indebted to Bob Pearson of Marion Allen Insurance, an insurance company that insured me at one time, whose insights about lawsuits in the inspection industry helped to inform this book and whose wisdom increased my understanding. Also, I'm grateful to many inspectors who shared their stories with me and allowed me to tell about them. They are wealthy, in the true sense of the word, when compared to those who extorted money from them in frivolous lawsuits, for they are poor indeed. Where justice and the courts have failed we can only hope that the law of karma is still at work and will prevail.

Table of Contents

Chapter One

Chapter Two

Chapter Three

Chapter Four

Chapter Five

PREFACE

The title of this book is intended to reveal its theme and its content, which is about the many ways to inspect properties and avoid lawsuits and disputes. I'm a professor of literature and intended to teach for a living, but due to circumstances beyond my control I elected to give up teaching and become a general contractor, after which I became a residential and commercial building inspector. I retired at the end of 2016 but spent more than twenty-five years as an inspector, and despite my experience I don't regard myself as a master inspector, or a master of anything for that matter. What I've written about grew out of an unpleasant experience with lawsuits that I chose to share with other inspectors in the hope that they might avoid a similar fate. If my experience has taught me anything, it has taught me that some states in our union are extremely litigious, and particularly the state in which I did business, and that many inspectors have been victimized and had their livelihoods jeopardized by a legal system that is easily corrupted. Justice is an ideal and a noble one indeed, but it's an ideal nonetheless.

Many years ago, the Los Angeles Times reported that real estate led the nation in litigation, and I was not surprised. I speak of lawsuits throughout this book, not only because it threatens the livelihood of inspectors but because I've been one of its victims. In fact, if I hadn't been unjustly sued more than once this book would not have been written, and I wouldn't have become the owner of a report-writing software company, which I allowed to be sold in 2008 to get rid of a crooked business partner. However, it's important for me to identify myself as the current co-owner of SwiftMark software and the author of a dozen inspection-related libraries, because I truly believe that report-writers with sophisticated libraries are the foremost protection against lawsuits. Indeed, significant parts of this book explain in detail why this is so. Regardless, if my experience can help even one person to become a better inspector or avoid a lawsuit this book will have served its purpose. Nevertheless, litigation will remain a threat to inspectors, because there'll always be people who are willing to profit at the expense of others and in any way they can. We cannot hope to change these people, but we can change ourselves and the way in which we inspect and report on properties. I know, because I have done so, as you will see.

CHAPTER ONE

The Law and Lawsuits

Mother Teresa dedicated her life to serving the poor, and will likely be canonized as a saint. [She was canonized after this was written, on 4 September 2016]. In the last few years of her life she and the nuns of the Missionary Sisters of Charity set about to build a shelter for the homeless in the South Bronx, and when two of the nuns found a Madonna in the rubble of a burned out three-story building, they likely believed that providence had ordained the site. In the spirit of charity, Mayor Ed Koch sold them the property for one dollar, and with five-hundred thousand dollars in funds from the religious order the future suddenly looked brighter for the homeless, but it was not to be. After months of bureaucratic drudgery and with approved plans and work already underway, the nuns were told that regulatory law mandated the installation of an elevator. They explained that their religious order prohibits the use of mechanical contrivances, protested the unnecessary expense, argued that only dormitories would be on the upper levels, and reasoned that the money would be better spent on food, clothes, and services for the poor, but the law was intractable and that was the end of it. The work came to a halt, and the homeless shelter never came into existence. The nuns graciously sent a letter to the bureaucrats thanking them for an education in the mysteries of the law and looked for other ways to continue their charitable work. If this case had not been documented by New York attorney Philip K. Howard in The Death of Common Sense (Warner Books, 1994), I wouldn't have believed that such madness and mindless stupidity was possible, but as Howard has carefully documented "modern law has not protected us from stupidity and caprice, but has made stupidity and caprice dominant features of our society" (p.185). Don't think for one moment that is an isolated case, because it is not. Because of such lawsuits and mindless stupidity, McDonalds and other fast food chains must now warn their customers that the coffee in their cups is hot. Yes, freshly brewed coffee is hot. Similarly, the District Attorney for New Jersey filed a lawsuit against Nissan North America alleging that the company failed to warn consumers that the expensive Xenon headlamps on the 2002 and 2003 Maximas were a favorite target for thieves. And, unbelievably, under a finders-keepers law in Florida a thief found himself entitled to money in the trunk of a car he'd stolen. Another thief found himself compensated for injuries he sustained when he fell through the skylight of a building he was attempting to break into and rob. Such legal madness is enough to try the patience of a saint, let alone we mere mortals.

Such legal oddities may seem remote from our lives as inspectors, but they're not. Just because you may not have been sued increases the statistical probability that you will be. I did business in California, where inspectors are liable for the properties they inspect for four years, and while real estate agents have an ethical if not a quasi-legal responsibility to pass on inspection reports to every Tom, Dick, and Harry that shows an interest in a property, these same people have the legal right to sue us whether or not they have a contract with us or have paid for our services. This flies in the face of common sense, but it's written into case law. In another case that confounds common sense, an inspector in California was sued over a pool that didn't exist at the time of his inspection, and another was sued by someone stupid enough to dive into the shallow end of a pool from the top of a water slide and cripple himself. One inspector expressed the opinion that it was nature's way of cleansing the gene pool, but it also expressed his frustration about how easily we can be victimized by morons, scoundrels, and the law itself. Another inspector was sued for an allegedly dust-contaminated furnace that his report indicated needed to be cleaned, and I was sued over something that was disclaimed in my standards and specifically disclaimed in my report, and by persons who'd never met me, never had a contract with me, and had never paid even a dime for my report. And, what's worse the innocent are dragged into lawsuits along with the guilty. Under the doctrine of "equitable indemnity" everyone is included in a lawsuit until they pay an attorney to get them out of it, which is a guarantee of easy money for a whole tribe of attorneys.

Equitable indemnity can be seen as reasonable and just, as it was when it was first applied. It stemmed from a motorcycle case that stipulated that consumers were entitled to rely on the reports of specialists. For example, if I paid to have a motorcycle serviced by a specialist and then sold it to you with the itemized receipt for the work you'd have the right to rely on the information even though you hadn't actually paid for it. That's fair enough, right? In this instance, yes, of course it is, but to make that a law is stupid. And you can understand what that means for you and your inspection reports, and how easily you could become a victim of the law. What Howard argues is that the law has replaced humanity: "we have constructed a system of regulatory law that basically outlaws common sense," he says (p.11). And he goes on to say that we've all but abandoned the application of the British common law, which takes the circumstances into account, as well it should. He reasons: "The accident caused by swerving to avoid the child is excusable; falling asleep at the wheel is not. The most important standard is what a reasonable person would have done" (p.23). Remind yourself as you read this book that "the most important standard is what a reasonable person would have done," because most of the lawsuits I'm familiar with have nothing to do with reasonableness or common sense, but instead have been totally unreasonable as you will see over and over again. Believe me, I never went looking for cases to confirm this and never ever encouraged anyone to tell me about their lawsuits, and when attorneys themselves acknowledge such madness, as I'll show they have, we can be assured that the system has indeed been corrupted by stupidity and greed and that we're at the mercy of blue-collar criminals protected by our legal system. So, how could this have come about in a country in which we celebrate our freedoms?

It began centuries ago when America adopted the British legal system and all but abandoned the concept of British "common law." It's from this fundamental concept that the jury system evolved; a system that's predicated upon common sense and a system that guarantees that the circumstances of an alleged crime will be heard and judged by a jury of our peers, but don't look for that common sense standard of justice today. Philip K. Howard's remarkable book confirms what many of us inspectors have rapidly had to learn the hard way: "Modern law has not protected us from stupidity and caprice, but has made stupidity and caprice dominant features of our society" (p.185).

Rest assured that it was never my intention to seek out bizarre lawsuits that denigrate the legal profession and confound common sense; such lawsuits have simply become commonplace in our industry. As I've mentioned, I've been sued over something that was specifically disclaimed in my standards and specifically in my report and by persons who weren't even my clients. Such lawsuits make all of us helpless victims of the law, and threaten our livelihoods as inspectors. Everyone that I told about my case was as dumfounded as I was. It was difficult for me to believe that it was even possible. One or two people may have thought I was making it up or perhaps not telling the whole truth, but most literally shook their heads in silent amazement. Of course, I turned the case over to my insurance company and paid my deductible and a file was opened, and thus began a process of perfectly legal extortion. Shortly thereafter, I received four identical "form" letters from my defense team, all dated on the same day, that reminded me about the limitations of my coverage and warned me of the possibility that my "personal assets could be looked upon to satisfy any judgment or verdict." I understood that it was their duty to apprise me of my rights and even understood their use of the bland euphemism "looked upon" to describe a very real threat to my livelihood, but I was hoping for something more positive, that someone on my defense team was feeling outraged about an obviously bogus case and a flawed legal system and offer me some words of comfort. However, it forced me to "look upon" my modest home and vintage English sports car in a very different light; not as physical extensions of myself and my family but as "personal assets" that could be legally seized in the name of the law. Resigned to my fate and determined to better protect myself, I spent the rest of the day humming: "Ain't that America home of the free, baby," an old song by John Couger Mellancamp. You might be wondering about the outcome of the lawsuit, so I'll tell you. It was settled for economic reasons as I knew it would, and more money found its way into the pockets of scoundrels and my life went on much as it had before, but is that justice in the land of the free and the home of the brave?

Who's Looking Out for You?
According to The National Center for Tort Reform, civil lawsuits have increased more than thirty-two percent over the last fifteen years, or at the time I wrote this, and building inspectors have contributed to this statistic. Bob Pearson of Marion Allen Insurance confirms that twenty-five percent of all inspectors are sued and, to make matters worse, a high percentage of the lawsuits are frivolous indeed. Nigel Bonny, who's an attorney and the General Counsel for FREA Insurance, reports in an article published in *Florida's Inspection Voice*: "at least seventy percent of claims that reach my office are without merit," and San Diego attorney Mark D. Stavros says the same thing, in *Mediation: Anecdote to Legal Abuse against Home Inspectors,* in which he writes: "While there are a number of lawyers who prosecute actions with merit, there are nonetheless a significant number of cases pursued in bad faith." Attorney Kris Thompson says something similar in the September/October issue of CREIA's *The Inspector,* but adds: "You must be ready for a lawsuit even on an inspection where you did everything right." This is the truth and bleak news indeed, and especially when we consider that these are attorneys making these public statements and not a few disgruntled or angry inspectors.

None of this would matter if inspectors could count on justice being served but they can't, and the sad truth is they're virtually powerless to do anything about it. Therefore, I was pleasantly surprised years ago to hear President George Bush call for the need for tort reform, and not shocked to hear Bill O'Reilly, in his book Who's Looking Out For You (Broadway Books), (p.166), describe our judicial system as a "cesspool of corruption." O'Reilly can be overly dramatic and I'm certainly not among his fans, but the average inspector is certainly aware that the real estate industry has been corrupted for years by frivolous litigation, and which continues to threaten the livelihood of every inspector in the nation. Even the liberal Los Angeles Times confirmed that real estate is the "most litigious issue" in America today. But, nothing has changed.

Regardless, this sad state of affairs is not limited to just the inspection industry, as can be inferred from the titles of two books by New York attorney Philip. K. Howard, one of which I've already cited: The Death of Common Sense: How Law is Suffocating America (Random House) and The Collapse of the Common Good: How America's Lawsuit Culture Undermines Our Freedom (Ballantine). Regardless, there's absolutely nothing that inspectors can do to prevent litigation, nothing. And until there is some meaningful tort reform, or until common sense predominates in our courts, inspectors will have to learn how to avoid litigation or become one of its victims. To that end, bear in mind that I'm saying "avoid" and not "prevent," which is impossible, but I'll share some plain truths with you. These are the facts.

Most inspectors are sued because they have deep-pockets in the form of their errors and omissions insurance, which makes them attractive targets. And the vast majority of the lawsuits are settled for economic reasons, regardless of whether the inspectors are guilty or innocent. You can't blame the insurance companies, because they're in the business of making money and, it could be argued, have no moral or judicial responsibility. However, by not defending the innocent they perpetuate injustice, and even though we may not like it we can understand why after a little legal wrangling, to dignify the process they settle almost every case. For example, why would an insurance company spend one-hundred thousand dollars or more to defend an innocent inspector when they could settle a claim for thirty-thousand or so? However, let's suppose you're sued and lucky enough to be honorably defended and even win, which is most unlikely, what have you won? The lawsuit will have cost you the price of your deductible, you'll have a case on your record, your premium will likely increase, and you'll have spent a lot of time in depositions with attorneys when you could have been doing inspections and making money or spending time with your family. Regardless, all inspectors bear the cost in higher premiums, but let's consider some other reasons why inspectors are sued.

First and foremost, inspectors remain liable and vulnerable to a lawsuit for every property they inspect and, depending on the statute of limitations, for as long as four and even five years, and yet they're only on-site for a few hours at most. Furthermore, although inspecting a property may seem simple, it's a very complicated process that can takes years to master. The knowledge that's necessary to perform a competent inspection has filled many books. But let's just suppose that all inspectors possess encyclopedic knowledge, such knowledge would be useless unless they could spontaneously recall each and every detail and communicate them effectively. And, of course, none of us possess the memory or the skill to do that. And, few inspectors can match attorneys when it comes to language skills. In fact, in this regard, the average inspector is simply no match for the average attorney. But it wouldn't make any difference anyway because as I've said after a few legal exchanges to dignify the process, most cases are settled long before they get to court. And even if a case does get to court, we can't assume that justice will be served. So what can be done?

The solution can be made to seem extremely complicated by those with a vested interest in maintaining the status quo, and there are many and include those who make the law and those who profit from it. However, there are simple solutions, but they're cumulative and not absolute. The first obvious line of defense for inspectors is their contracts and standards. These documents are continuously being revised and improved by the best minds in the business, but they won't do inspectors any good unless they're sued for breach of contract, which is highly unlikely, or until their case goes to trial, which is also highly unlikely. It's worth repeating that nothing can prevent litigation, but there are many different ways to avoid it. First and foremost, what every inspector needs is a report-writer and a sophisticated library that contains thousands of industry-standard narratives that have been as carefully prepared as our contracts and our standards, narratives that can be edited, added to, and polished each and every moment if necessary. After all, a computerized report-writer is basically a mechanism of storage and retrieval that's capable of containing an endless amount of information that can be retrieved with a few simple clicks of a mouse. Such programs enable us to generate sophisticated narrative reports that not only educate clients about things of which they know little or nothing, but which are comprehensive enough to help us avoid disputes and litigation. Let me give you two examples of how a computerized report-writer can help to avoid litigation. Both examples came about as a result of lawsuits that are part of the public record.

An inspector in California was sued over the death of a child who'd climbed on a tall fountain and pulled it down on herself, and was killed instantly. Of course, the inspector's standards disclaimed an evaluation of landscape components, but that didn't stop the lawsuit. After hearing about it, I was haunted by the knowledge of the tragedy and imagined how devastated the parents must have been and how shocked and powerless the inspector must have felt. And then I began to think about all the properties I'd inspected that had heavy concrete fountains and bird baths, and about which I'd said nothing. And thinking about concrete bird baths and how common they are, I imagined a toddler in diapers holding onto the edge of one and straining to see inside, but then I banished the image of what might happen next. However, I realized that with a computerized report-writer I had the means to avoid a similar potential tragedy and lawsuit by including a general disclaimer and a specific narrative for every conceivably dangerous item on-site, including this one for fountains which I added to my report-writer: "The landscaping includes a pre-cast concrete fountain, which I did not evaluate and disclaim. It consists of heavy, stacked, components that pose a safety-hazard, and particularly to children. Therefore, the fountain should be adequately secured or removed." I added similar narratives for ponds, cascades, bird baths, concrete benches and statuary, all of which stipulate the need for action and disclaim further responsibility. This is what contemporary jargon terms "being proactive," but I didn't want to depend on standards. I wanted to educate my clients, serve them well, and possibly avert a tragedy and a lawsuit.

The second example is drawn from a case that was certified for publication by an appellate court in California, Moreno vs. Sanchez, case number B145698, a lawsuit in which an inspector was sued by a client/attorney for illnesses or allergies that were allegedly caused by a dirty and rust-contaminated forced-air furnace, which the inspector had reported needed to be cleaned. Whatever the perceived merits of the case, I thought that it was outrageous, and as soon as I'd finished reading it I checked my own report-writer to confirm that I had plenty of narratives that recommend a cleaning service for various reasons. Then, I added one that can be checked to print automatically, which I hoped might provide a first-line of defense against a similar lawsuit:

We do not test for indoor air pollution, which the Consumer Product Safety Commission rates fifth among potential contaminants. Nevertheless, inasmuch as health is a personal responsibility, we recommend that you have the indoor air quality tested as a prudent investment in health and environmental hygiene, and particularly if you or any member of your family suffers from allergies or asthma.

It's a shame that we have to remind adults that they're responsible for their own health but some clients and most attorneys need to be reminded, and if it prevents one inspector from being sued it's worth it. There are literally thousands of narratives like this in the report-writer, and you're welcome to any that appear in this book. Regardless, until you can count on the judicial system to look out for you, you should be looking out for yourself and, remember, help can be just a click away. If this sounds like someone trying to sell libraries, so be it. However, I never try to sell them and only allow someone to buy them. And that just happens to be the truth, the whole truth, and nothing but the truth, so help me God.

A Tale of Two Attorneys

At a CREIA conference in California, I spoke with several inspectors, who'd read a couple of dueling articles between me and a local CREIA attorney that involved inspectors who were willing to admit they'd been sued. The sad truth is that none of us want to publically admit we've been sued, because it's embarrassing and demeaning to be sued. In many ways, it's analogous to a dirty family secret that we're ashamed to talk about except in private, which is exactly what attorneys would like, because the real truth is a national shame and a disgrace to the legal profession. Regardless, there are other equally sad truths, such as the fact that once we've been named in a lawsuit we've lost even if we happen to win, which is rare indeed. I might be one of the few inspectors talking publically about this, and believe me it wasn't easy, but many inspectors feel outraged and utterly helpless. However, I must admit that one of my fellow inspectors once described my articles as "tirades," but that's okay. He was smiling when he said it, and what a dull place the world would be if we all felt the same way. Besides, the word "tirade" is derived from a word that means "to draw, and fire," and I'm ex-military and have a fondness for weapons and words and cherish the true meaning of the word. Regardless, I fully expect to hear from even more outraged inspectors, but let me tell you a tale of my own, a tale about two attorneys that would be comical if it wasn't real.

A few years ago, I walked into the office of a plaintiff's attorney ready to be deposed as one of several defendants in a bogus inspection lawsuit. The receptionist was surprised to see me, and said that my deposition had been postponed and assumed that someone must have forgotten to inform me. Anyway, the attorney overheard me announce myself and hurried into the reception area. "Swift," he said, raising his arms in welcome, "I've heard some interesting things about you, and I'm delighted to meet you" he added, extending his hand and smiling. I'd arrived with a chip on my shoulder and ready for a fight, so his warm greeting caught me off guard. "I've heard some interesting things about you," I replied, staring directly into his eyes, "you're purported to have said that good lawyers don't clean their teeth in the morning they sharpen them." He chuckled, and before long, we were lounging in the reception area and chatting amicably about the lawsuit like old soldiers. He was a veteran attorney, and cautioned me that he shouldn't be talking to me without my attorney being present, but I assured him that I didn't need my attorney present to state what I thought were unequivocal truths about the case and my innocence. I even told him that the expert witness he'd commissioned was a falling-down drunk who'd avoided a construction fraud case by plea-bargaining, which he obviously didn't know. In fact, few inspectors knew about it, even though his public drunkenness was well known. Weeks before, I'd provided my attorney with the transcript of the Los Angeles Superior Court lawsuit involving him and couldn't wait to see the addle-minded expert witness exposed in court for the socially degenerate mercenary that he is. Perhaps the attorney appreciated my honesty, which obviously gave him the opportunity to replace his expert witness before the trial, but after a few more minutes of verbal sparring he jumped to his feet, extended his hand, and declared: "You don't belong in this case, Keith. Have your attorney call me in the morning, and we'll see what we can do about getting you out of it." Knowing what I've said about attorneys, that honorable gesture earned my respect. I should also admit that before that moment I'd actually entertained a few homicidal fantasies about him, his alcoholic expert witness, and his sleazy clients.

I hurried home to my beautiful wife to boast how I'd single-handedly slain a dragon, but settled on the truth and told her that the plaintiff's attorney was a charismatic and intelligent fellow whose brief company I'd enjoyed. Then, overjoyed, I immediately called my attorney and left a jubilant message on his answering machine proclaiming my victory. So what did he do? On the following morning without consulting me, he sent an email that berated and threatened the plaintiff's attorney for daring to discuss the case with me outside of his presence and promptly turned my victory into a disappointing defeat and left me locked in the lawsuit. From that moment on, the plaintiff's attorney wouldn't even acknowledge the calls I made to thank him, and who could blame him? The case dragged on for almost two years while the attorney's fees continued to mount on both sides. My insurance company finally agreed on a settlement, and either went out of business or cancelled my policy; I can't remember which. As for my attorney, I'd become somewhat friendly with him before that incident and for the longest time he continued to invite my family to join his for dinner. And, who knows, we might have become friends, but I just couldn't bring myself to break bread with a man who'd betrayed me. I'm the type of man who says what he thinks, and that wouldn't have made for pleasant dinner conversation in front of our wives. Later, I also politely declined to inspect a house for him for the same unspoken reason, but for those who may be inclined to believe that I have no respect for attorneys, nothing could be furthest from the truth. In fact, if you haven't guessed already, New York attorney Philip K. Howard earned my respect and admiration many years ago, and I encourage anyone who has an interest in justice and the common good to do what I did, which is to buy multiple copies of his best-selling books and give them away as presents. We should never forget that justice is worth fighting for, and those attorneys who tell the truth and honor justice are worthy of respect, and those who don't are beneath contempt and beyond help or hope.

Perfectly Legal Extortion
Many years ago, I attended a dinner meeting at a local chapter of California inspectors and was keeping to myself. I was not a member of the chapter or the organization, and was not keen on joining for personal and philosophical reasons that aren't important. Anyway, I'd been doing inspections for about five years and was seated at a round table with other inspectors, including one celebrated for being "the inspector to the stars," who asked me if I'd been sued, and when I told him I hadn't he just shrugged and without looking up from his plate mumbled: "You will." I smiled, but the truth is I really didn't think that I would. I'd learned my trade with my hands, and thought that I probably knew more about the trades than he, but he was right and shortly after I was victimized by a frivolous lawsuit. "Pride goes before a fall," or so teaches The Book of Common Prayer but I had to learn that for myself the hard way. Many of the cases I've become familiar with involved inspectors who didn't wish to their names to be made public, and for which reason I'll share one with you in which I was victimized and which will illustrate what I mean. Everything that I'm going to tell you is the truth, the whole truth, and nothing but the truth. But, if you want to read it, it's Los Angeles Superior Court case EC040173. This is how it began.

I went to my mailbox late one afternoon and found a tin of home-made cookies with a note from a grateful client, and also a summons. The cookies were a joyous surprise, but the summons was a shock. I consoled myself with a couple of cookies, and went home to review my report and reread the charges against me. I won't bore you with the details, but this is what I discovered. I was being sued over something that was disclaimed in my published standards and again specifically in my report, and by persons who weren't my clients and who'd never paid for my service. Once again, I kissed my deductible goodbye, and forwarded the lawsuit to my insurance agent, who forwarded it to their adjusters, and thus began a process of perfectly legal extortion. A week or so later, I was invited to an on-site meeting by an adjuster, which I immediately declined. This must have surprised him, because within ten minutes my attorney called and seemed equally surprised. Other inspectors must have been more cooperative, but I wasn't about to participate. As far as I was concerned, it was a legal charade, which I wasn't going to waste my time on or condone with my presence. However, I did point out that I was indisputably innocent and being railroaded, and I had no intension of wasting my time by participating in a legal process that I predicted would end once a decent amount of money had been assured would change hands.

The onsite meeting took place without me, and a few days later I received four "form" letters from my legal defense team, mentioned earlier and all on the same day. I was hoping for a more positive touch, and amused to get four identical letters warning me that my "personal assets" could be "looked upon" to "satisfy a judgment." Lawsuits are all about words, and I happen to be interested in words and pay close attention to them, so let me explain how these phrases were carefully chosen so as not to awaken the primitive animal that lurks just beneath my skin and that of most civilized people. For this same reason, professionals choose their words carefully. For instance, a surgeon might explain that "an incision will be made in your abdomen," but he certainly wouldn't say he's going to "cut open your belly," and legal professionals are no different. Subjects are concealed with the use of the passive voice instead of the active, and the real meaning is hidden in Greek and Latinate words instead of more simple Anglo-Saxon ones. Consider these phrases quoted from the form letters: "looked upon," "personal assets," and "satisfy a judgment." They consist of abstract words that don't name things that exist in the real world, in the way that concrete words do. And, what they attempted to do was to disguise a real threat to things that I cherish. Can you imagine what I might do if I was told that someone might try to take the modest house I'd rebuilt after an earthquake, and the classic Jaguar I'd lovingly restored, or the money I'd worked hard to save over the years? That threat could unleash some primitive animal instincts that I'd be hard-pressed to control, believe me. And, remember, the people who are telling me this are on my side and part of my legal defense team. But let's get back to the lawsuit. However, rather than bore you with the details of the case and my opinions, I'll prove what happened by sharing actual emails between me and my attorney, with names omitted. As I am sure you'll agree, these emails leave absolutely doubt that I was being railroaded by a lawsuit that had nothing to do with truth and justice and everything to do with money changing hands. But, consider the emails and you can judge for yourself.

From: [Name omitted], Wednesday, April 20th, 2005 12:00 PM
This will update you re this water intrusion/mold suit to advise that [Name omitted] has completed her investigation and concluded that this is a limited to no liability matter based among other things on the fact that the assured disclosed that his inspection excluded common areas including the east exterior wall which appears to have been the

source of water intrusion into the unit. [Name omitted] advises that mold abatement is completed but reconstruction hasn't begun. The claimants' alleged loss is $58K (although continuing since they have not returned to the unit) and [Name omitted] estimate is closer to $17K. Co-defendants including the HOA so far are denying liability, are just starting to enter appearances in the case, and the HOA counsel says they won't be prepared to mediate until they get further discovery. We've advised opposing counsel that this is a no liability case subject to summary judgment but he has refused to dismiss although he is supposedly consulting with his clients re possibly resolving the claim against the assured. Subject to instructions to the contrary we'll file an answer by tomorrow's deadline and issue a written discovery set in an attempt to move this towards a dismissal and we'll advise further if and when we receive any kind of demand from opposing counsel. This is probably another claim where if we don't get a dismissal shortly we can file a summary judgment motion without waiting for discovery responses to put added pressure on the claimants to drop the claim against assured. Thanks, [Name omitted].

The "assured" refers to me but, regardless, I hope as you read this you noticed there's no mention of the fact that the plaintiffs are not my clients and never paid for my services or my report. This vital information didn't appear in the case documents either. Where's the justice in that? There are other mitigating facts that confirm my absolute innocence, but I won't go into them. However, read on and you'll see how I feel and how I actually predict the outcome. An uncommon word appears in the next email, "chicanery," which I chose carefully confident that my attorney would understand. It means "legal trickery."

From: Keith Swift Wednesday April 20th, 2005 4:26 PM
Dear [Name omitted]: Thanks for the info. I'd like to say that I'm grateful, but I'm still appalled by this chicanery. In days gone by when men were men, if you'll excuse the stale metaphor, the plaintiffs and their attorney would be hung up by their thumbs, or set in the stocks for a few days and pelted with tomatoes or rotten fruit. Such was the glory of the common law. One day, when the case has been settled for economic reasons—as we both know that it will—and a sufficient amount of money has changed hands, I'll tell you what I'd like to do. But, rest assured, I'm a civilized man, albeit a pissed-off civilized man.

From: [Name omitted], Wednesday, April 20th, 2005 7:50 PM
Thanks Keith, and you're probably right re where this is ultimately headed but only time will tell and if we throw a decent amount of sand under their wheels early we may just convince them you're more trouble than you're worth (so to speak). Thanks again, [Name omitted].

I didn't reply but received this blunt email about three weeks later, which didn't include my first name and wasn't as warm and friendly as the others:

From: [Name omitted], Tuesday, May 10th 2005 7:01 PM
This matter settled today at $8,000.00 with the assured's verbal consent and conditioned on good faith, etc., with payee info to follow once we get it. Thanks, [Name omitted].

This is what is meant by the euphemistic phrase "resolving the claim," which is a skillful way to sanitize legal extortion countenanced by the court. I was tempted to end this account with the last blunt email, and let the exchanges speak for themselves, but as I'd predicted in the beginning the case would never go to court and would end when enough money had changed hands. It's a joke, and yet one more case that has made a mockery of justice. Call it what you like, but it's perfectly legal extortion, plain and simple. Do I understand why the case was settled? Yes, of course I do, and if I was in the insurance business and only cared about money I might do the same thing, but does that make it right? I felt like Cool Hand Luke, in the movie of the same name, as he was being stripped of everything except his underwear and locked in a box about the size of an outhouse, and for no offense whatsoever. A guard apologized to Luke as he handed him a latrine-bucket, saying: "I'm just doing my job, Luke." To which Luke replied: "That don't make it right, Boss." Are attorneys just doing their job when they file frivolous lawsuits against innocent inspectors? This lawsuit happened many years ago in 2005, and I'm still angry. It's not in my nature to be a victim or to admit defeat. The lawsuit cost me, and it ultimately cost all inspectors in increased premiums. Some inspectors may even be forced out of business by the repeated legal assault by people who are no better than criminals, and that term certainly applies to the sleazy plaintiffs and their attorney in this case. However, for those of you who have never experienced legal extortion, it is torture. Interestingly, "torture" and "extortion" come from the same Latin word "tortus", which means "to twist and inflict pain" and that's what it was like. And, there was absolutely nothing I could do except grit my teeth and bear it and then soldier on.

What Do You See?

Inspecting any property is a serious business, and a risky one. The reasons for this are complicated. Most of us carry huge amounts of money in the deep pockets of our errors and omissions insurance, which makes us attractive targets, and a courthouse is not always a forum for justice but a place in which huge amounts of money change hands. Unscrupulous people can file frivolous and even fraudulent lawsuits without any fear of being punished. And they can usually count on insurance companies to offer them money to simply go away. With nothing to lose they're encouraged to sue, and they do. It's a disgrace. But there are less obvious reasons why inspectors are sued, which are rooted in human nature. Many people that have a home inspected don't know anything about them. They don't know why water comes out of a tap, or what warms a house in winter or keeps it cool in summer, and they really don't want to know until something goes wrong. Then they tend to remember that it was inspected, and believe that an inspector must somehow be responsible. And when this happens, the truth can vary from person to person. Let me show what I mean with three pictures taken from within a foundation crawlspace that I inspected many years ago. In the first picture, you can see an abandoned and open floor duct that could allow dust into the living space, and

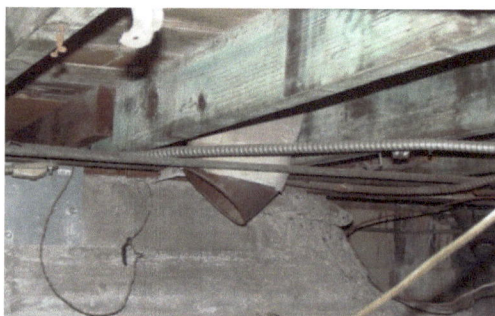

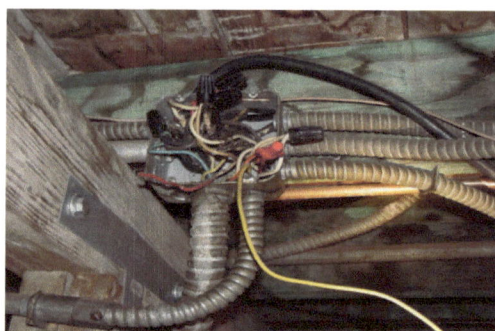

14

which also has a paper seal known to contain asbestos. In the second picture you can see an open and miswired electrical box, and in the third picture the rusty trail of an old drip-leak on a galvanized water pipe. However, what many attorneys might see in the first picture is an open duct polluting the living-space with a known carcinogen that's capable of causing lung cancer and an excruciatingly painful and lingering death, and in the second picture an open, overloaded, and miswired electrical junction box ready to arc and spark at any moment and burn the house down with an innocent family trapped inside, and in the third a leaking pipe capable of promoting a whole colony of life-threatening biological organisms. And, they're also likely to allege that these commonplace deficiencies have caused their clients extreme emotional distress, undermined their faith in humanity and condemned them to a lifetime of existential dread that only a million dollars can cure. And I didn't even bother to mention that the floor joists had been treated with copper naphthenate, which is also an alleged carcinogen.

Poor communication contributes to many lawsuits. The word itself comes from a Latin word that means "to share," and that's what inspectors should strive to do. Unfortunately, too many inspectors rely on their contracts and standards of practice for protection, but that's a mistake. Inspectors are generally sued for negligence and rarely for breach of contract, which pretty much nullifies all standards and the legal mumbo-jumbo of all contracts. Let me give you an example from a case that was certified for publication by the Appellate Court of California. An attorney and his wife made an offer on an old house, which the owner declined to sell to them when he learned that the husband was an attorney. However, under the threat of being sued the sellers agreed to sell the house and provided a lengthy and detailed disclosure about everything they knew about it, including its defects. After living in the house for a while, the attorney and his wife developed what were alleged to be chronic respiratory ailments, and after hiring specialists to test the air quality and failing to discover anything they were able to find a mercenary HVAC contractor who was willing to testify that the conditioned air was being contaminated by dust. So what did the attorney do? He sued the inspector.

The inspector had attempted to limit his liability to the inspection fee, which didn't work, but that's another story. If you want to read the case, instead of relying on my opinion, the Los Angeles Superior Court case number is BC218733, but it will probably make you angry. Could the lawsuit have been avoided? Yes, I believe it could. The inspector should have made sure that his report informed his clients about potential contaminants, reminded them that health is a truly personal responsibility, and cautioned them to have the air quality tested and the ducts cleaned as a wise investment in environmental hygiene. This may sound like the type of verbiage that a specialist might include in a report, and if it is so be it. It's better to spend a few hours adding informative and cautionary narratives to a report-writer, which can be included with a simple click of a mouse, than weeks and months dealing with crooked clients and corrupt attorneys. But what other ways are there to avoid being sued?

First of all, let's agree that a negligent inspection is indefensible. But, what's a competent inspection and can a generalist perform one? When I did my first inspection, my equipment consisted of paper check-sheets I'd compiled after lifting ideas from every report I could get my hands on, a ladder, a flashlight, two screwdrivers, a measuring tape, a pair of pliers and an outlet tester, which was a recent acquisition that I hurried home to show my wife. "What's reverse polarity?" she asked, turning it in her hand and looking closely. "I'm darned if I know, darling" I replied, "but it's not good." We still chuckle when we remember that moment. Now, I'm a certified deal-killer, which isn't true, but you know what I mean. I have my own report-writer and a sophisticated library, a digital camera, and several thousand dollars of specialized equipment, and the truth is I wouldn't do an inspection without them. Of course, I'm aware that a laser level could be said to be an engineering tool that could jeopardize my standing as a generalist, but I could care less about standards when it comes to protecting myself, and I'm convinced that it has probably saved me from a few lawsuits. So how can we best avoid being sued? It's by having the earnest desire to communicate or, in other words, the willingness to share. I'll illustrate this with another tale from the trenches. By the way, the tales that I tell throughout this book are real, not imagined. However, I despise tall-tales and gossip and would never tell anyone's story without their permission.

An inspector was threatened with a lawsuit over alleged structural damage that was said to exist in a forty-nine year old house that he'd inspected several months earlier. When the inspector returned to the house, he noticed that an extensive renovation was underway; carpets had been removed, walls had been opened to expose framing and some were in the process of being removed. His once friendly clients were now distant and aloof, and were merely allowing him to see the alleged defects to satisfy a clause in his contract that guaranteed him the right to do so. However, they did condescend to point to an eighth-inch crack in the slab and a three-quarter inch cold-joint separation between the slab and the footing and called his attention to a musty odor. He attempted to render an opinion, but they weren't interested. They already had the opinion of a so-called expert and an estimate for repairing the slab, which left the inspector alone to contemplate his fate. Two weeks later he was sued for alleged negligence, but before the case went to court his insurance carrier settled the case for fifteen thousand dollars. It cost the inspector his twenty-five-hundred dollar deductible, his premium was subsequently increased, and he'll never know whether it was because of the particular case or because of the cost of others like it. One way or another, the cost of insurance is passed on to every inspector with insurance.

You're probably thinking that the inspector had no way of knowing about the condition of a slab concealed by carpet and that his clients should have realized this, for which reason industry standards deem an inspection to be essentially visual and disclaim things that are not visible. That's also because you're applying common sense and probably believe that all legal decisions are fair and reasonable, but many inspection lawsuits are anything but reasonable and have nothing to do with common sense. So how might this lawsuit have been avoided? The inspector should have communicated better. Instead of relying on his contract and industry standards as a means of protection, the inspector should have accepted the responsibility of educating his clients and protecting himself and warned them specifically about the very real possibility of cracks being found in an old slab foundation. As for the musty odor, the pungent smell of soil will certainly penetrate slab cracks, and anyone who removes carpets and opens up walls in an old house should expect to experience them. Nevertheless, the inspector should have also realized that people are not necessarily rational or honest. If you want my opinion, the plaintiffs found a guaranteed way to have their inspector assist in the cost of renovating an old house. Let me explain how this lawsuit might have been avoided, but in a roundabout way.

Grading, drainage and moisture-related problems are among the leading cause of lawsuits, and particularly those involving older houses with slab foundations. For this reason, every report should include a description that prints automatically of an ideal site that has hard surfaces, roof gutters, area-drains, soils that slope away for a distance of six feet, a difference in elevation between the exterior grade and the interior floors and, ideally, a French drain that receives and conveys water around a house. The narrative should include a disclaimer disavowing responsibility for any site that doesn't meet the ideal. My site evaluation begins with the blunt statement: "Water is destructive," and goes on to explain how water can find its way into even the tiniest cracks. I've never had one client disagree, but the disclaimer probably bothered one or two real estate agents who saw the closing of their escrow threatened or delayed by my reports.

Avoiding a lawsuit is analogous in some respects to a boxing match, which is rarely won by a single uppercut or right-cross but by an accumulation of jabs and body shots before the knockout punch. In this respect, the subject of avoiding lawsuits is complicated, and my views may seem overly simplistic, but I do believe that the answer lies in better communication. And by that I don't mean adding narratives to a report that are commonly described by agents and attorneys as "boilerplate," but narratives of indisputable facts that educate. Justice follows truth, or should, and there's nothing more disarming than the plain truth. But, let's consider some other ways of avoiding lawsuits.

CHAPTER TWO

Defending Against Litigation

I've spoken to enough people at conventions and chapter meetings to know that well-trained inspectors are ambushed daily by attorneys. It's a threat that we live with, and the reason why we carry insurance. However, most inspectors continue to believe that it won't happen to them. It's like the myth of immortality that most of us believed when we're young. And, please believe me when I tell you I never thought I'd be sued either, but I was. And even when we're inclined to admit that we might be sued, we're confident that justice will prevail if not all the time most of the time, which is also not true. Attorneys bend the truth every day, and insurance companies are far more likely to settle a suit for economic reasons than defend innocent inspectors. But, let's say you're sued, honorably defended, and even win, you've still lost your deductible, you've lost a lot of precious time, and you risk losing your coverage. So, what have you won? Let me give an example of how this can happen to anyone by paraphrasing what I said to an attorney when I was told that my insurance carrier was about to settle a bogus mold case against me, which had dragged on for almost two years and which I'll tell you about later. "So what you're telling me," I said, "is that I've paid a $2,500.00 deductible to settle a lawsuit against me for alleged negligence in failing to alert my clients to a fungus that we can actually prove didn't exist at the time of my inspection and which I identified, and which according to industry standards and state regulations I'm not even supposed to comment on. And what about the fact that the plaintiff's ignorant attorney couldn't get my name right and even misidentified me as the owner of a termite company? You call that justice?" There was a moment of silence, after which the attorney agreed that the decision had nothing to do with justice, and explained that his hands were tied. It would have cost the same amount to file a motion for a summary judgment, he explained, and with no guarantee that a judge would grant the judgment the insurance company had decided to settle. It may have been a prudent business decision, but it sure taught me a lesson in life that I was to learn again. However, this is not simply an isolated or unusual case. In fact, such cases are a commonplace, and are threatening our livelihoods. If you haven't learned this already, I hope that you will by the time you've finished this book.

Inspectors may not be aware of how many inspection-related lawsuits are filed, simply because they're self-reliant and proud individuals who don't run around telling each other: "Hey, Guys, I've just been sued." It's obviously embarrassing to be sued, besides which complaints are commonly overstated to make inspectors seem like blithering idiots or, worse, mass-murderers. Attorneys are notorious for such hyperbole. In addition, the lure of easy money and not a passion for justice drives many of them. And this is true of most of the complaints I've read, which were overstated or woefully inaccurate. And the sad truth is that the attorneys on both sides don't seem to give a damn; they remain in cahoots while the costs continue to mount. Remember, I've already showed you how my own attorney kept me involved in a lawsuit from which I'd been released, and it too was not an unusual case. And, I've already told you how the indisputable facts in a case against me were never acknowledged by anyone, including my attorney. At the risk of sounding self-righteous, I was probably the only one telling the whole truth. It was as if my attorney didn't want to embarrass the plaintiff's attorney by pointing out blatant factual errors. Isn't that negligence? If it isn't, I don't know what it is, but attorneys always manage to get away with such deception. So, don't expect justice, or anything approaching that ideal. What inspectors are facing is tantamount to terrorism, or at least that's how I came to regard the threat to my livelihood and I've acted accordingly, and I hope you will too. In fact, I entitled one of my articles *"Terrorist Are Among Us,"* and they certainly are!

First of all, inspectors are likely to find themselves outnumbered by a legal team of attorneys and expert witnesses with specialized instruments. And, with rare exceptions, these so-called experts are actually mercenaries who'll fight for whatever side is paying them. I've read a few reports by so-called expert witnesses, who I would love to question under oath. Their depositions showed them to be fools or liars, or both, but few lawsuits ever get to court where one still hopes justice will prevail. Therefore, I've elected to carry weapons that are at least as sophisticated as theirs. I'll go into greater detail later, but I'll give you one example of how useful such weapons are in avoiding lawsuits. I was inspecting an old and very expensive slab-on-grade residence that had less than ideal drainage conditions, but nothing that appeared to threaten the interior. There was moisture damage to the base of a laundry room wall that backed up to a bathroom with a stall shower, and also similar damage several feet away in a hallway, both of which I reasoned could have migrated from the shower area and been drawn up into the plaster by capillary action. However, a series of moisture meter readings continued to lead me further and further away from the stall shower and on down a hallway, In fact, I ultimately reasoned that the shower pan probably wasn't leaking and that moisture was actually penetrating the slab from below. Of course, this wasn't what the visual evidence seemed to indicate at first. And, remember, the standards of practice restrict us to what can be seen. Regardless, to cut to the end of the story, I recommended further exploration, implied that destructive testing might be necessary, and which in fact revealed even more damage and led to a geological survey that confirmed that the damage was being caused by an ancient spring or aquifer that was contributing to extremely high moisture content beneath the house, and which proved that the slab had the equivalent value of a reed mat laid over a swamp. Would a lawsuit have resulted? I don't know, but without the evidence of the moisture meter readings I wouldn't have recommended destructive testing, and if I hadn't a multi-million dollar lawsuit could have resulted in which I would have likely been branded as a criminally negligent fraud who'd willfully and maliciously jeopardized the lives of countless innocents. And, please don't delude yourself by thinking that industry standards would protect you because they won't. You won't be sued for breach of contract, but for negligence. Ask anyone who has been sued. But let's consider other powerful weapons besides moisture meters that can protect us.

The best weapon by far is a computerized report-writer. To continue with the military metaphors, they're like wearing a flak helmet and body-armor. And let me warn you that if you're still using recorders or check-sheets, typing out individual reports, or printing a report on-site you're an exposed and stationary target, because they only offer the equivalent protection of a paper shield against an AK47. It doesn't matter how much you know or how skillful you are, you can't possible retain and recall all the knowledge you need to protect yourself. And the beauty of a computerized report-writer is that it allows you to continuously refine and polish your reports to give better and better protection. Here's one admittedly insignificant example. A few years ago, I got an email from a client/attorney berating me for not having warned him about the potential for bacterial infection lurking inside the pipes of his hydro-spa. The truth is that it had never even occurred to me. I wrote back, saying that there'd been no evidence of bacterial residue when I filled and ran the hydro-spa, which was true. Then, I explained that he probably hadn't used the spa for a while, and reminded him that I wasn't responsible for his poor housekeeping. Thank goodness, I didn't hear from him again but you can see what I'm getting at. Now, thanks to that email exchange with an attorney I'm better prepared and and every one of my hydro-spa evaluations includes a narrative that prints automatically and warns about bacterial residue and recommends periodic flushing with an anti-bacterial cleanser, as well as testing its ground fault protected circuit. Of course, I'm not suggesting that anyone would be likely to forget a complaint from an attorney, and I relate the story only to make a point about memory. For instance, how many of us can remember every water heater, every window, and every furnace that's been recalled, or how much and at which point framing members can be safely notched? But such information can be at our fingertips. And, believe me, I'd be too scared to go into the field without it, because ever since my first encounter with the enemy inspections have come to mean a continuous preparation for the next mission and terrorist attack. Let me give you another example from my own experience, and one that was a little scarier.

I was hired to inspect a magnificent property in the Santa Monica Mountains overlooking the Pacific Ocean, and I was almost finished when the friendly seller informed me that because the builder had been slow in responding to some requests for changes when the house was new he'd hired a construction defect expert to evaluate the residence and shared the report with me. It was sixty pages long and alarming, and I only had chance to skim it. It recommended that the copper water pipes be removed and replaced, because of an alleged patina on the outside of some. I was aware that flux is corrosive and runs down from a fitting that's being soldered, and if it's not immediately wiped away with a damp cloth it can cause a greenish patina. This is not always done effectively because the pipe can be burning hot. However, an eddying process at fittings that weren't de-burred can also contribute to a patina and even predicate a leak. In fact, I have a narrative in my report-writer that cautions my clients about this rare possibility, but I was unable to confirm any patina on the visible portions of the pipes. In addition, the expert recommended that the stucco be removed and that all the dual-glazed Andersen windows be replaced, which he predicted would leak. I had no idea how he'd arrived at these alarming conclusions, but that was only part of his report. Needless to say, I immediately added a narrative to my report that referenced his and stated that I was not endorsing any component or condition that he'd identified as needing service or a second opinion. This so-called expert would obviously be a powerful asset to a prosecuting attorney, and he certainly had me ducking and running for cover. Regardless, let me share with you what I sometimes refer to as my first-line of defense.

Every different section of my reports begins with a substantial narrative that prints automatically and is designed to educate my clients, reasonably limit my liability and, hopefully, confound attorneys. It's followed by general narratives that have the same purpose but with a narrower focus. Together, they form a powerful first-line of defense. Of course, one can never know what defenses work best until they're tried. However, I truly believe that a combination of such narratives can prevent an attack, but they'll only serve as pressure bandages to stop the bleeding once you've been hit. Remember, the best defense is an offense. For this reason, inspectors need to have an arsenal of narratives in a report-writer that can be fired like bullets at anything that's threatening. For example, how many inspectors could name all the brands of allegedly defective ABS pipes, let alone the specific batch numbers of those predicted to fail? And how many could identify the water heaters with defective burners that were sold under different brand names, or those that have dip tubes made with defective polymers that will self-destruct? And how many inspectors know the permissible spans of rafters and joists, and where and to what extent they can be notched? The truth is, not many. But detailed technical information like this can be stored in a sophisticated report-writer. Also, what about Chinese drywall, and the defective materials and components in all the other systems that we evaluate? Even knowing something doesn't help if you don't remember or can't recall it, but the step-by-step process of selecting and evaluating components in a report-writer will not allow you forget, and that's the beauty of a report-writer with a truly sophisticated library.

Inspectors are willing to accept the risk of evaluating hundreds of diverse components and conditions, but very few are blessed with photographic memories and instant recall, and most of them simply couldn't hope to match wits with a team of attorneys in a battle of words. And the truth is, although I'm no expert and certainly not qualified to give legal advice, I've been out there for a long time. I've been shot at and missed, and even hit a couple of times. And there's nothing more gratifying in life, they say, than being shot at and missed, but even if you're hit there's usually no warning. You'll find yourself down, and wondering what the heck happened. Anyway, you're probably growing tired of all the military metaphors by now, so let me end this part by asserting that inspecting a property is like entering a war zone. So if we want to survive, or until we can boast of a judicial system that passionately defends truth, justice, and the common man, we really do need to have camouflage, body armor, sophisticated weapons, and all the ammunition we can carry. Now, let's talk specifically about specialized instruments.

Specialized Instruments
The use of specialized instruments, like the quotation of codes, has caused dissent among inspectors. Some argue that their use can jeopardize our status as "generalists," while others point out that nothing in the standards prohibits their use. One thing is sure however, inspectors are fascinated by them and always gather around tool booths at conventions. Interestingly, I've read arguments against their use, including one article that defined a spirit level as "specialized engineering tool," but I still favor them because they help to avoid lawsuits. First of all, I don't believe their use jeopardizes our standing as generalists, and as difficult as it is for me to say anything positive about litigation in the inspection industry I don't believe an inspector will ever be blamed for going beyond the standards. But even if this is disproved the trick is to avoid litigation, because as I keep repeating once you've been named you've either lost or are in harm's way. I know, because my policy was cancelled even though my attorney wrote a letter to the carrier confirming that my two lawsuits were settled for economic reasons and not because of negligence on my part. Regardless, "negligence" and "fraud," are the most powerful words in an attorney's arsenal, because they can pierce the shields of our contracts and our standards. Ask any inspector who's been sued whether it was for breach of contract, negligence or, worse, fraud. Besides, insurance companies are like tin men in one respect, they don't have hearts but they do have bulging wallets.

For many years, my only defense was common sense, a contract written in plain English, paper check-sheets, a ladder, a measuring tape, a flashlight, a screwdriver, a pair of pliers, and an outlet tester that I would never fully understand and regarded as something mysterious, like lightening. I lived in a make-believe world of sweetness and light, in which justice and truth prevailed, and it took a couple of lawsuits to ground me firmly in the real world. This is what an attorney told me, and what he'd tell you: "You've got deep pockets, in the form of errors and omissions insurance, and you're going to be sued. So, get used to it. It's the cost of doing business." Isn't that hard to accept? Anyway, that's when I began to add more specialized instruments to my arsenal of weapons. Yes, they're weapons, because it's a war zone out there and prosecuting attorneys are like camouflaged snipers with sophisticated telescopic rifles and laser-guided bullets. When you're hit, you won't hear the percussion or see the muzzle flash, you'll just find yourself down and wondering what happened. The trick is to keep moving and out of their line of sight, and a computerized report-writer together with specialized instruments can help you do that. I'll illustrate this with two more tales from the trenches.

The ear is a truly sophisticated instrument that includes a microscopic fluid-process that transmits messages to the brain through nerves and hair-like structures called cilia, which alert us when we're not straight and level. That's how we can sense when a floor slopes, but it's not foolproof. Many years ago, I was standing in the entry of a relatively new three million dollar house and overheard a flooring contractor telling my clients that he didn't need to use his level to confirm that the floor was "way out of level." The price of the house is not important, and I relate it only to make the point that people who can afford to pay three million dollars for a house can certainly afford to hire an attorney to sue an inspector. Anyway, as I stood in the entry listening, I looked around and saw a cathedral-like area bathed in light with a marble floor and vaulted ceilings. I looked carefully and didn't see anything out of the ordinary, and I was not convinced about what I was hearing. The openings looked square, and given the quality of contemporary building I never expect to find perfectly square openings or perfectly level floors. Regardless, and after setting up my equipment in the kitchen, and aware that no one was paying attention to me I placed my self-leveling laser-level on the floor and confirmed that it was indeed five-inches out of level. I was shocked, not because it was out of level but because, as the floor contractor had said, it was significantly out of level. My clients declined to buy the house, and I was not told why, but I did hear later that it continued to fall out of escrow and eventually became the subject of a lawsuit. The flooring contractor and of course my laser level helped me to dodge that bullet, and I learned further that several geologists had confirmed that the soil in this desirable area of multi-million dollar homes is expansive and, therefore, subject to movement. The truth is I never take out my laser level and wave it around for everyone to see, but it's always with me. And, of course, a new narrative was added to my report writer about this area.

Here's another tale from the trenches. The house that I was inspecting was old, but had been totally renovated. It was about fifteen hundred square feet and vacant, and I was left alone with absolutely no pressure on me whatsoever. The listing agent opened it and, after asking me to lock it up when I was finished she assured me that it was a "cream puff" and predicting that I wouldn't find anything wrong and left. It was Friday, and I was looking forward to taking my wife out for dinner. I'd just about finished and found enough deficiencies to convince myself that I'd provided a worthwhile service, when I decided to shoot elevations with my laser level. The living room, dining room, kitchen, and a corner bedroom in the front were found to be well within tolerable limits for an old slab-on-grade foundation. Then I shot elevations down the carpeted hallway and on through an old master bedroom addition in the rear, which were fine until a point at the where the addition began at the end of the hallway and at which point the slab sloped dramatically, or approximately three inches out of level in fourteen feet. Reasoning that if the slab had settled that much there had to be evidence of movement that had to have been apparent at some point and then concealed. The old single-glazed windows had all been replaced and the stucco was new with no evidence of stress or movement. The attic entrance to the addition was inside a walk-in closet, where I noticed the ceiling had been patched. So I went back into the attic to a point above the closet and pulled back a fiberglass bat and confirmed breaks in the plaster. Then, I closed the attic and pulled back the carpet in the closet, and found a slab separation at the point of the addition filled with non-shrink grout that confirmed movement. However, this had not been obvious on the outside or anywhere else for that matter. The addition was old and probably had an inadequate footing and had settled out of level years ago. Did I dodge another bullet with my expertise? No, I credit my laser level with yet another victory.

I could tell you many more tales from the trenches that make the same point, but the truth is even an ordinary flashlight is a specialized instrument. Let's face it, how many inspectors could explain the nature of lumens or the propagation of light? I know it will always remain a mystery to me, along with the inner workings of my outlet tester, my laser level, my infrared thermometer, my deep-probe moisture meter, my carbon monoxide detector, my digital camera, and my computerized report-writer. I'm still mystified by love, and happy to be so. For everything dissolves into mystery, doesn't it? And if we can only stop attorneys and their clients from assaulting us with frivolous lawsuits, we could sit around and ponder the real mysteries of life, or maybe just enjoy a glass of wine or a cold beer. You'll notice that I haven't mentioned infra-red cameras, but they're the penultimate specialized instrument and will revolutionize the industry.

Taking Pictures

To cite and old cliché, a picture is worth a thousand words. In fact, I've stated on many occasions that apart from a computerized report-writer pictures offer the best defense against lawsuits. Some inspectors agree, some disagree, and some have correctly pointed out that pictures significantly add to the length a report and increase its file size. However, I'm not suggesting that inspectors should photo-document everything, but they're a powerful means of non-verbal communication and can assist in avoiding litigation. In fact, photo-documentation can provide the best defense when reporting on things that are in perfect condition and don't need service. For instance, there could be a long-shot picture of a pool with its light on, followed by a picture of its ground fault protected circuit. Similarly, one could have a picture of an electrical panel with its dead-front off and one or two more showing that it's neatly wired and that its wires and breakers are matched, which would dispute any subsequent claim to the contrary. An inspector that I know has been photo-documenting for years but not necessarily including all of them in a report. I was entertained at a dinner-meeting one evening when he related that he once listened patiently while a money-demanding client berated him for not having reported that a pool light didn't work, and which the client claimed a pool maintenance man purported "had never worked." When the client was finished ranting the inspector politely asked him for his email address, and within a few seconds the pool light was shining miles away on his client's computer screen with the date of the inspection. I could relate many stories like this, and take delight in every one, because a digital camera is a truly formidable means of defense. I've dropped mine a few times, but it's shockproof and waterproof to a depth of fifteen feet and costs less than two-hundred dollars, so I don't mind buying a new one every year or so.

Personally, I cannot conceive of doing an inspection without my digital camera, which I use very methodically. By this I mean I tend to do the same thing in the same order on every inspection and take pictures as I progress, which of course makes them easier to enter in the report. I won't comment on the virtues of habit or repetitive behavior, but I can't let leave the subject of photo-documentation without sharing two of my favorite chimney photos, which I took a few years ago. The house I was inspecting had been almost entirely rebuild. In fact, only part of a foundation and a garage wall remained.

The first picture shows a brand new fireplace with an elegant hearth and surround. The second picture shows a close-up of its shiny new chase-cap and mat-black shroud. Then, you'll probably notice the absence of the flue, which terminates inside the attic butted up against the roof sheathing. These defects are hard to miss, but they illustrate why inspectors need to be self-disciplined. This wasn't apparent from the ground, and it would've been easy for me to tell myself that the roof was new and that I didn't need to access it. And, it would have been equally easy for me to view the attic and its brand-new components from the top of my ladder at the access, but my military discipline compelled me to walk the roof and enter the attic. Besides, how else could I confirm that the flue had fire-stop around it on the attic floor? And, imagine what might happen if I hadn't. The first fire in this fireplace would have likely smoldered unseen in the attic, filled the house with smoke, and erupted into an inferno. Just thinking about it gives me the willies. Interestingly, the roof, the chimney, and everything else had been signed-off and given a Certificate of Occupancy by an inspector from the local Department of Building and Safety and, believe it or not, the builder had the same so-called specialist who installed the chimney return to install it correctly. What can be said?

The Truth? Generalists or Specialists?
The truth about almost anything can be difficult to determine, but it's commonly established by numbers, authority, or tradition. In other words, we tend to believe some-thing is true if enough people say it is, or if a sacred text or a prominent authority says it is, or if it has remained unchanged for generations. However, this still doesn't mean that it's the absolute truth. What I've noticed is that most people tend to remember the simple truths they learned as children, and many try to live by them in the hope that the world will become a better place. Indeed, the truth is often plain and simple, so simple in fact that even children can understand it. So when I hear someone spouting a lot of fancy words I begin to suspect that they're either insecure or trying to conceal the truth. But what has bothered me most in recent years is to see how the plain and ordinary truth, or what most of us refer to as common sense, is ignored in our courts, ignored in the one place where we expect to hear it spoken and where it should prevail in the interests of justice. And this has to do with words, and explains in part how inspectors are victimized.

I've read quite a lot of lawsuits and rarely found one that demonstrated the beauty of the language and common speech, or one that had simple words and were a pleasure to read and easy to understand, let alone one that spoke simple truths. Attorneys seem to favor Latinate words over plain old Saxon ones. For instance, they say "cease and desist" instead of "stop." They must think that Latinate words and phrases sound more important and that the people who use them must therefore sound more intelligent, but nothing could be further from the truth. However, the truth in most lawsuits, and indeed in the law itself, is often smothered by Latinate diction in convoluted sentences that's called "obfuscation," and is typically as ugly and obscure as the word itself. There's no point in giving examples of this here. If you're interested, read George Orwell's celebrated essay "Politics and the English Language" or try to read and understand any lawsuit for that matter. Most include ridiculously overstated accusations and cluttered nonsense that totally obscures the meaning as well as the truth. For that matter, try reading an insurance policy. Orwell claims that "the great enemy of clear language is insincerity," and having read a number of lawsuits I certainly agree. Regardless, let's look at the truth as it relates to inspectors.

For several decades, industry standards have defined inspectors as "generalists," but what does that mean and is it the truth? There's no doubt that when the industry was in its infancy this label was intended to sensibly limit an inspector's liability. But, regardless, based on the many lawsuits I've become familiar with, I can assure you that clients and attorneys and indeed the courts regard inspectors as "specialists," in other words the exact opposite of "generalists" and not without good reason. The truth is we've come a long way since the early days, and most of us are specialists. We've studied and worked long hours to become professional inspectors, and along the way most of us have bought thousands of dollars of sophisticated equipment and specialized instruments. Besides, calling ourselves "generalists" has never stopped us from being named in a lawsuit or dragged into one. Attorneys don't care what we call ourselves. As I said earlier, I was dragged into a lawsuit in which the attorney didn't get my name right, misidentified me as the owner of a termite company, and omitted material facts, and yet was still able to extort thousands of dollars from my insurance company. I was totally innocent and told the truth, but that didn't matter. If you care to read the case, it's on file in the Superior Court of Los Angeles, number BC 263791. I'll tell you more about it later, but let's talk about the future for inspectors.

To repeat, most of us really are specialists, plain and simple, but this doesn't mean that we have to start doing things differently, start dismantling furnaces, lifting roof tiles, and opening up walls. That's invasive testing and most specialists don't even do that. HVAC specialists commonly service components without crawling under a house or into an attic to look at the ducts, and geologists don't take core samples every time they evaluate the soils on a property. It just means that we've got to reconsider what we are and what we do, and perhaps even rewrite our standards. I made the mistake of suggesting that a few years ago and thought I might be lynched. Change is glacially slow, but our industry is evolving and adapting, and in some states inspectors will be licensed whether they like it or not. I can think of arguments for and against it, but the idea is not without merit and licensing could enable us to align ourselves with other professionals and could actually reduce litigation, but this will certainly be resisted by those with a vested interest in keeping things as they are. Having said that and until there's tort reform, we must mount our own defense. And, no one can stop us from raising our voices as well as our prices, and being as professional as the so-called specialists. In the simple words of an ancient aphorism: "First the feathers, then flight."

Contracts and Standards

A few years ago, I attended two conferences on opposite sides of the country. At the first on the east coast, an attorney was booed when he was introduced as the guest speaker, and even though the boos were likely intended for comic effect the sentiment was clear and I felt sorry for him. His entire talk extolled the virtues of our contracts and our standards. At a question and answer period following his talk, I stood up and told him that multiple lawsuits I'd read had proved beyond any doubt that our contracts and our standards afforded little or no real protection and at best might result in a pyrrhic victory if a case ever went to trial, which is rare indeed. I was among strangers on the east coast, but my comments produced immediate and resounding applause, which made me feel even more sympathetic toward the attorney who simply nodded thoughtfully in response, but I did want inspectors to hear at least one other version of the truth. Many inspectors approached me afterwards to thank me and to tell me their stories, but for years many of us were reluctant to talk publically about such things. In fact, we still are.

At the second one on the west coast, a CREIA conference, I was approached by even more inspectors, many of whom knew me and several had read one or two of my articles published in their magazine "The Inspector," and who complained bitterly about lawsuits, including one against a high-ranking inspector and industry leader that was so utterly frivolous as to defy belief. These inspectors had also read an article of mine that came out in their magazine just before the conference, and they sought me out to share their horror stories, as though to show solidarity or confirm the truth about what I'd written. Without exception, they all thanked me and made me realize that I was not the only one who was hopping mad, and that our combined experience represented more proof that a disease as serious as cancer was afflicting our industry. Such stories are now commonplace, as more and more lawsuits spread like a disease for which there is no simple cure. Of course, many inspectors have not been infected but, unfortunately, it's only a matter of time. It's a numbers game, it really is, but there's always hope.

Most of the lawsuits I've become familiar with have been a war of words that had little to do with the truth. Decent attorneys who remember their oath to serve justice will admit this. For instance, one decent attorney, Mark D. Stavros, who I quoted earlier, had this to say in an article entitled "Mediation: Antidote to Legal Abuse against Home Inspectors?"

With relative efficiency, lawyers representing disgruntled home purchasers can recover a significant settlement against sellers, the inspection company, and the real estate agents with measured demand letters, calculated posturing, threats of fees recovery, and discovery fishing expeditions. While there are a number of lawyers who prosecute actions with merit, there are nonetheless a significant number of cases pursued in bad faith. By merely paying the filing fee, anyone can file a lawsuit. It ends only by a settlement, summary judgment or trial – rarely by flat dismissal.

Remember, this is an attorney saying this, and while I admire Mark's willingness to speak out against injustice, or what he correctly terms in the title of his essay as "legal abuse," the phrase "bad faith" strikes me as a bland euphuism with which to characterize attorneys who pursue cases without merit. Such attorneys are no better than criminals, and deserve the universal contempt that they've brought upon their own profession. Regardless, I'll be the first to admit that I've never been able to understand how a profession that depends so much on the power of words can have so thoroughly fouled the language. Can it be that they're not sincere, and that "the great enemy of clear language" really is insincerity, as George Orwell asserts? If attorneys wrote the traffic laws, none of us would stop at red lights; we'd cease and desist, and be too intimidated to drive on. Mark makes a good argument for mediation in his article, and I'm sure we could learn from him, but my intent is to discover ways to avoid litigation before it even gets to mediation. Besides mediation has nothing to do with determining truth but about seeing how much someone's willing to pay to get out of a lawsuit. In truth, I took the mediation clause out of my contract because I won't waste time playing games with attorneys. Anyway, the right words can help us avoid litigation. However, there are no words that can rationalize a bad inspection, and there shouldn't be; when inspectors are negligent they should expect to pay. That's justice, and when insurance proves its worth, but we do expect to be defended when we're innocent, and not have our carriers and attorneys make settlements with crooks to save money. It's wrong, and it's rotten.

The words in our contracts are our first-line of defense, but the contracts that I've looked at seem to be getting more and more bloated with impenetrable nonsense. Here's an example, written by an inspector who refers to himself as a "consultant," for reasons known only to him, but he probably fancied himself as being intelligent or wanted to sound like an attorney:

Consultant does not turn on, or otherwise cause to [be] activated, any gas-fueled utility, nor light gas-pilots or activate any gas-fueled appliance not functionally in service at time of observation.

I added "be," which was missing, but there's little point in commenting on the errors in this bloated nonsense, and there's little point in trying to understand why the inspector would resort to such cluttered communication unless in a stupid and misguided attempt to make himself sound more intelligent. I'm much too civilized to reveal the name of the buffoon who wrote this contract, but it's the same chain-smoking falling-down alcoholic that I mentioned earlier who was scheduled to testify against me as an expert witness. Anyway, the average person usually gives up trying to read such gibberish as this, and some even question their ability to understand it instead of questioning the intelligence of the person who wrote it. Contracts and other legal documents should be written in language plain enough for the common man to understand and, as I've mentioned, it's not without significance that "common" and "communicate" come from the same root word that means "to share." It's my guess that most industry contracts arise out of group meetings and then committees, after which they're transliterated into legalese by attorneys, which I suppose is intended to confer some sort of ultimate legal authority upon them. I've never understood this, but then again I've never questioned it before either. I've always trusted that if I'm called before the bench that a judge trained in the humanities or a jury endowed with common sense might appreciate the common-place language in my contract. But I've also hoped that it would never be tested, because the trick is to avoid litigation. Here's a small example of something that I think works. There's a clause in my contract that my clients are required to initial, which reads:

I agree that any recommendations that Keith Swift Inspections may make for service, a second opinion, or permit research shall be completed and documented before the close of escrow or Keith Swift Inspections shall be held harmless for any subsequently alleged defects or deficiencies.

The clause isn't exactly plain English, or as I originally wrote it, because an attorney I respect urged me to include the legal phrase "held harmless," and it seemed as much metaphoric as legalese so I was happy to oblige. Anyway, I believe this clause is entirely reasonable, and one that a reasonable person would be happy to initial. I've shared this clause with other inspectors, and some graciously accepted it as a gift. However, one inspector who read it and who apparently shared in the creation of an industry contract, became quite indignant and assured me that a similar clause had been suggested before and been unanimously rejected by eminent legal advisors on the grounds that it was merely an attempt to indemnify inspectors against prosecution. Regardless, I'd rather walk away than argue with a zealot, and particularly one who had something to do with an industry contract, so I did walk away without a word. However, this rather ordinary clause is not intended to indemnify me against prosecution, it's intended to make a client reflect for a moment on what's reasonable and fair and call me before they pick up the phone and call their attorney. Regardless, I'm confident that it works because most people are fair and reasonable and if it gets thrown out in court what have I lost and what does it matter? However, this doesn't mean that I approve of every clause that attempts to limit liability. At the risk of annoying some inspectors, let me say that I regard any clause that seeks to limit liability to the inspection fee, or some small multiple thereof, as shameful. I've seen a few and said nothing, but would you sign a contract with such a clause? I wouldn't, and do you think that promising to refund the inspection fee would satisfy the owner of the house shown below, which was inspected?

Before we continue with our discussion of contracts and standards, you're probably eager to hear more about this house. It's relatively modern, as you can deduce from the shear-paneling beneath the torn felt paper, and it didn't collapse in an earthquake but moved glacially slowly for several months, in fact long enough for me to notice when I occasionally drove by that the cracks were becoming more pronounced. As it turned out, the ultimate collapse was caused by rains invisibly lubricating the soil. Interestingly enough, the house had been inspected one or two years earlier but not by me, and although I would have reported the cracks as evidence of structural movement and recommended a structural or geological evaluation, I could never have predicted such a catastrophic failure. Regardless, I'm happy to report that there was no loss of life and that a father and his two young children escaped from the house, alive. It will remain in this sorry state until a lawsuit is resolved. You might want to make a mental note that this house was indeed inspected before it collapsed, and it's quite possible that you'll inspect one just like it in the future. So, don't ignore cracks, even seemingly insignificant ones, but let's get back to the subject at hand.

Many of the words and phrases in industry standards are as sterile as those in industry contracts, and typically consist of a series of declarative phrases beginning with the words, "the inspector shall observe" or, conversely, "the inspector shall not observe." Surely inspectors would be much better served by a detailed account in plain English of exactly what we do and what we don't do, and why. I won't cite anything from specific standards to illustrate what I mean, because it might imply an organizational bias that I certainly don't have. To me, all standards are the same or similar, and all could be improved, and we're all in the same boat when it comes to being sued, so let's just consider a standard that might read something like this, which I'm not endorsing and only using as an example to make a point: "The inspector does not lift carpeting, or move furniture and other personal items." This is concise; no question about it, but it's of little value to a client and even less value to an inspector. Here's a story from the trenches that should illustrate what I mean, but remember the value of the phrase "does not lift carpeting" as a means of defense because, by itself, it's worthless.

A doctor and his second or third pretty young bride bought an expensive house, which they were having remodeled before moving in. The doctor is successful and makes a lot of money, but because of a recent divorce he's carrying three mortgages, the remodel is taking longer than he was promised and costing more than he'd anticipated, and the expenses are mounting every day. Nevertheless, his bride is happy so he's happy, that is until the morning she calls him in tears from their dream home to report that when the contractor removed carpet he found what he describes as "major damage" to the slab foundation, which he estimates will cost between twelve and fifteen thousand dollars to repair. The doctor drives home in a hurry, consoles his bride, and consults with his contractor, who tells him that his inspector should have warned him about such damage. He's upset, but being an intelligent man and realizing that his inspector doesn't have x-ray vision he doesn't know what to do. Later that day, he meets a friend at a country club for a game of golf, a friend who also happens to be an attorney and he knows exactly what to do. Need I tell you how the tale ends? However, let's go back to the beginning and tell the same story differently.

Realizing that slabs are prone to cracks, including cold joint separations that contour the footing and can be as wide as one-inch, commonly result from shrinkage, and have little structural significance, the inspector included some very educational information in his report, together with a recommendation for a second opinion:

This residence has a slab foundation. Such foundations vary considerably from older ones that have no viable moisture barrier under them and no reinforcing steel within them to newer ones that have both. Our inspection of slab foundations conforms to industry standards, which is that of a generalist and not a specialist. We check the visible portion of the stem walls on the outside for any evidence of significant cracks or structural deformation, but we do not move furniture or lift carpeting and padding to look for cracks, and we do not use any of the specialized devices that are used to establish relative elevations and confirm differential movement. Significantly, many slabs are built or move out of level, but the average person may not become aware of this until there is a difference of more than one inch in twenty feet, which most specialists regard as being tolerable. Regardless, many slabs are found to contain cracks when the carpet and padding are removed, including some that contour the edge and can be quite wide. They typically result from shrinkage and usually have little structural significance. However, there is no absolute standard for evaluating cracks, and those that are less than 1/4" and which exhibit no significant vertical or horizontal displacement are generally not regarded as being significant. Although they typically result from common shrinkage they can also be caused by a deficient mixture of concrete, deterioration through time, seismic activity, adverse soil conditions, and poor drainage, and if they are not sealed can allow moisture to enter a residence, and particularly if it's surcharged by a hill or slope, or if downspouts discharge adjacent to the slab. However, in the absence of any major defects, we may not recommend that you consult with a foundation contractor, a structural engineer, or a geologist, but this should not deter you from seeking the opinion of any such specialist and for which reason we disclaim any further responsibility.

I grant you that this is a lot for a client to read but it's educational and offers a better defense than stating "we don't lift carpets," and it has the power to prevent a lawsuit. But, for the sake of argument, let's say in this case it didn't because an attorney was involved, the inspector would still have a reasonable chance of having the lawsuit dismissed in a summary judgment. And that's what we need, a reasonable chance for justice to prevail, although preliminary judgements were designed to protect judges more than litigants. But, what we also need is standards that truly educate clients and contracts that protect us, contracts for instance that would guarantee compensatory damages for inspectors who've been victims of frivolous prosecution. But this will never happen as long as there's money to be made by attorneys and as long as our contracts are approved by attorneys and filled with the verbose and convoluted diction that bears little resemblance to the language of the common man. And this is a national shame, because what our country and our judicial system desperately needs for justice to prevail is common sense and fairness. But, don't look to those who write the laws and profit from them, or insurance companies for that matter.

CHAPTER THREE

Getting Started in Business

I'm often asked by inspectors that I've mentored what to charge for inspections and, of course, I've never been able to give them a simple answer; there are too many factors to be considered. I'd work for a loaf of bread if it meant feeding my family, and I might even steal one. Regardless, you should bear in mind that litigation is costing the real estate industry millions of dollars every year, and the cost is increasing. The good old days when deals were sealed with a handshake are gone, and have been since the early sixties when real estate agents began to be sued as though they were vagrants selling snake oil. Defenseless, and unable to attest to the condition of the properties they were selling, they naturally began to advise their buyers to seek the evaluation of specialists. Contractors saw a new market for their services and began advertising themselves as inspectors, and an industry was born. Many others followed, some less qualified, but all eager to meet a growing demand, and so the inspection industry flourished virtually unregulated. Organizations were formed and services became more standardized and thereby informally regulated. Despite this, litigation continued to increase; the only difference being that now inspectors were being sued along with the agents, while the attorneys gathered like vultures.

Faced with lawsuits, many inspectors simply went out of business, and agents and inspectors came to regard each other as adversaries. And, unfortunately, that has somewhat characterized their relationship ever since, and prevents them from uniting against the threat of litigation. In California, two or three major brokerage firms conferred and in an effort to limit their liability formulated lists of "approved" inspectors, who were somehow deemed worthy because they happened to have errors and omissions insurance and belonged to an organization of inspectors, which is the same as asserting that everyone that has a driver's license and insurance is a good driver. In turn, the inspectors closed ranks, compared war stories, and devised spurious new contracts with mind-numbing legal jargon designed to limit their liability, and all to no avail. Litigation continued to increase, along with the number of inspectors with deep pockets. If all litigation was fair and reasonable, or even if most of it was, there'd be no cause for alarm, but it's not. Innocent agents and inspectors alike are being sued every day, while more and more attorneys flock to the feast with their beaks agape. Meanwhile, despite attempts by various organizations to create a professional image for inspectors, the public sees embarrassing images displayed on national television that demean them. But, if you haven't seen them I won't say too much more.

Inspectors and real estate agents don't have a very positive image. Agents have long been stereotyped as being dishonest and in national surveys are ranked on a par with used-car salesmen. And most of what the public has learned about inspectors recently has been from embarrassing pictures of foolish ones displayed on primetime national television. Of course, the exposes were carefully edited to be more entertaining than educational, which is becoming characteristic of the sensationalizing media. But we shouldn't pretend that such negative stereotypes are completely unfounded. Some agents are corrupt and brand competent inspectors as deal-killers and others are simply foolish, and whereas some inspectors are merely incompetent others are truly negligent. But let's talk about the cost of inspections.

Where I did business, geologists and structural engineers typically charge eight hundred dollars for a verbal report and approximately twice that for a written one. Few inspectors charged anywhere near that and yet their responsibilities are far greater, and in some states their liability can extend for as long as four or five years. The reasons for this glaring disparity are obviously difficult to understand. Most inspectors consider geologists and engineers to be professionals, and even though their own services entail far greater responsibilities they don't seem to regard themselves as such, or if they did you'd think they'd demand similar fees. By contrast, realtors regard themselves as professionals, and have indirectly contributed to the negative stereotype of inspectors because, in spite of the fact that they receive a percentage of a residence's sale's price, they expect inspectors to charge a pittance based on its square foot size and not on its market value, which is illogical. Similarly, they commonly shop for discounted fees, and make it clear that they're not willing to read substantial reports, and typically brand inspectors that provide them as deal-killers. What they want to see are five to six-page reports with check boxes and chicken scratches from inspectors who are "realtor friendly," and we all know what that means, but let's just say what it means. It means that there are thousands of inspectors doing two or three inspections a day for a mere pittance, leaving themselves in legal jeopardy, and denigrating the professional image of inspectors nationwide, while pandering to thousands of real estate agents, many of whom don't give a damn about anything but closing an escrow.

Yet, in spite of rampant litigation and escalating insurance premiums, some inspectors foolishly regard any suggestion to restructure fees as price-fixing. Are realtors price-fixing when they expect and receive a percentage of the sale's price? I'm not prepared to suggest a uniform fee, but if I did it would certainly take into account that clients are not paying inspectors for what they do but for what they know. It would always take into account the market value of a property, the history of frivolous litigation, the duration of an inspector's liability, the rising cost of insurance, and the likelihood of being dragged into a lawsuit, and the strong possibility that it will be settled for economic reasons. So what is the true cost of an inspection? You might want to ask an attorney, but one of the potential costs is typically stipulated in almost every summons and complaint and reads: "To be determined at the time of the trial."

Meeting Buyers and Sellers

It's important to become acquainted with your clients, because it can actually help you to avoid disputes and even litigation. It's easy for people to get upset with their plumber, their mechanic, or their inspector, but they're less likely to get upset with a Joe, a George, or a Harry. Jonathan Swift said it best three hundred years ago when he confided to a friend: "I hate and detest that animal man; although I heartily love John, Peter, Thomas, and so forth." Experience has probably taught you this already, but it's worth remembering. Introduce yourself to your clients and include your first name, explain to them what your inspection entails and how long it's likely to take, and be sure to ask if there's anything they're concerned about, such as environmental contaminants. What you might learn is that they've fallen hopelessly in love with their dream home, and really don't want to hear anything negative about it. Like star-crossed lovers, they're inclined to regard a wart on the nose of their beloved as a beauty mark and the absence of teeth as a shy smile; that is until the honeymoon is over. Unfortunately however, you're there to report on the condition of the property and not to pander to their emotions or make realtors happy. After speaking to your clients for a minute or two, you might conclude that they have reasonable expectations or completely unreasonable ones. Regardless, be attentive to their concerns, but impress upon them the importance of reading the entire report, and assure them that you'll remain their consultant indefinitely. Remember, communication is important. As I pointed out earlier, it comes from a Latin word that means: "to share." Regardless, many veteran inspectors have confirmed that their first impression of a client significantly influenced the creation of their report. In other words, they documented things that their clients were concerned about far more carefully than they might otherwise have done.

Similarly, a client's first impression of you will either inspire confidence or evoke distrust. So have confidence in yourself, and make sure that their first impression of you is a good one. Regardless, it's essential to establish your authority but not in a brash or an aggressive way. Be respectful but firm and confident, and never allow anyone to tell you how to do your job. Many inspectors have politely declined to complete an inspection, and generally with good reason. A client once handed me back the contract without signing it and said: "I can see what you don't do, which is almost everything. So what the blank do you do?" I snatched the contract out of his hand, tore it in half in front of him and said, "I don't blanking work for you." My assistant could barely contain himself until we were back in the truck and moving, at which point he kept slapping his knee, laughing and praising me, after which he insisted on buying me breakfast. He knew he was going to get paid anyway, as well he should. It wasn't his fault that our client was a sociopath. We enjoyed breakfast, and he learned a lesson I'd never taught him before.

Sellers can be equally irrational and hostile. I once revealed a plumbing leak, which now seems quite comical. I was running a shower in a second story bathroom for a few minutes, to put the drain under pressure, which was still running when I heard a muffled shout from the ground floor. Moments later, the realtor came stumbling upstairs to tell me that water was dripping on the seller who'd been dozing in a recliner below. Moments later, he too appeared, breathless and indignant, with a damp T shirt. "What the hell d'ya think doing?" he blustered. When I explained that I was testing the shower, he became even more indignant. "That shower hasn't been used for twenty years," he snorted, "and if someone wants to shower they'll use shower downstairs." His response was completely irrational. Nevertheless, I listened politely and explained that it was my duty to test such fixtures whether they'll be used or not. He was not consoled and followed me around, glaring at me in sullen silence. I still smile when I think of him dozing and getting dripped on in his recliner. Thank God it wasn't a leaking toilet. However, it did teach me quite early on in my inspection career that people can be completely irrational, but enough of that. You'll probably hear hundreds of stories like this, if you haven't already, but it's not just irrational and hostile people that you need worry about.

A significant number of the complaints involving inspectors begin when dishonest contractors attempt to defraud consumers by first alarming them. These contractors typically warn of chimneys that are about to burn a house down, or furnaces that are poised to kill silently with carbon monoxide. In many cases, consumers have panicked, called inspectors, and berated them for not reporting such horrors. However, out of all of the horror stories I've heard over the years involving contractors warning of disasters, hardly any of them had any merit. Regardless, I actually caution my clients in a conclusion to my report that prints automatically about anyone using inflammatory or emotive language or who have a vested interest in alarming them, and urge them to seek a second opinion. And, naturally, I'm always happy to advise them and recommend reputable specialists but, alas, there'll always be people who prefer to believe the worst and others who prefer to have attorneys resolve their disputes by filing lawsuits.

Anyway, to continue, you should also take the time to introduce yourself to the sellers and to the real estate agents and present them with business cards. Be respectful and courteous, and remind yourself that your inspection is an invasion of the sellers' private space. You may even wish to explain to them exactly what your inspection entails and assure them that you'll be respectful of their property and will leave it in exactly the same condition you found it. Remember, the sellers could become your clients and your allies, and if they respect you they might share information with you, such as the age of the roof or the details of its maintenance history. Also, don't forget to ask them first if they have any animals you need to be concerned about. I once spent the better part of an afternoon trying to capture a skittish Poodle I'd allowed to escape from a back yard, and some years later I spent a few terrifying seconds being pursued by a Rottweiler before I scrambled to safety over a wall.

Inspections are really all about communicating, except when attorneys become involved, and then it's about anxiety, verbose and convoluted language that the average person couldn't hope to understand, and astronomical amounts of money changing hands. And yet verbose and convoluted language is what passes for communication in our legal system, and there's really nothing that you can do about it. So place your faith in your own ability to provide a competent service and trust that others will grant you with the same respect and dignity you show them and, yes, save a little money for a rainy day.

Home Protection Policies

In the state in which I did business, sellers are encouraged by real estate agents to purchase a home protection policy for the buyers and usually do. The policy costs them about three hundred dollars, and gives the buyers the false sense of security that if anything goes wrong with the house after they've purchased it all they have to do is call the insurance company who sends someone out immediately to make repairs or replacements for a modest service fee. Nothing could be further from the truth. Nevertheless, many real estate agents continue to use home protection policies as a sale's tool. "You don't have to worry about anything," I've often overheard them say to buyers during the inspection, "because if anything goes wrong all you have to do is pay a forty-five dollar service fee and they'll come right out and repair or replace things." But what really happens? When something does go wrong, as it will in every house in America, the homeowner calls the insurance company, a representative arrives and after collecting the fee for the service call usually finds some reason to refuse service. "It's a code violation or a pre-existing condition," the representative commonly asserts, "which is disclaimed in the policy." And they're notorious for adding that the home inspector is really at fault for not having warned them. And, naturally, the next call is to the inspector. I don't know whether this is a common occurrence in other states, but I can think of many times in my area when this has happened to inspectors, and not one of them had any merit. After responding to several similar quasi-complaints from clients, I concluded that it was my duty to better educate them, which I did with a narrative that prints automatically in the conclusion of my reports. Since then, I've only received one or two calls involving a home protection policy, and as soon I read to them or remind them about the advice given in my report, they either agree that things had indeed transpired exactly as I predicted, or graciously thanked me for the valuable advice. Of course, I always offer my support, and advise them how best to get the service they deserve. Here's the cautionary advice I leave my clients with:

You should not regard this inspection and report as being a guarantee or warranty of the property and its components. It is not. It's simply a report on the general condition of the property at a specific point in time. Furthermore, as a homeowner, you should expect problems to occur; roofs will leak, drain pipes will become blocked, and components and systems will fail without warning. For these reasons, you should take into consideration the age of the house and its components and keep a comprehensive insurance policy current. If you've been provided with a home protection policy, read it carefully. Such policies usually only cover insignificant costs, such as that of rooter service, and the representatives of some insurance companies are very likely to charge you for a service call and then deny coverage on the grounds that a given condition was preexisting or not covered because of an alleged code violation or a manufacturer's recall. Therefore, you should read such policies very carefully, and depend upon our company for any assistance and consultation you may need.

You're welcome to use this, but I hope that you never have to depend on it. However, I do believe it has the power to stop nuisance calls and maybe even lawsuits. However, let's talk more about inspecting properties.

CHAPTER FOUR

Inspecting Properties

I'm early to every inspection, and regard the practice as the start of a reconnaissance mission on which I study the lay of the land and anticipate where I might be ambushed. Call it paranoia, but it keeps me on my guard and makes me view a property as a war zone and a house and its components as potential booby-traps. This is how I begin all my inspections, including one that I did a few years ago. The house was vacant and had been recently renovated, which made me more cautious. There was an old slab-on-grade addition in the rear with little or no difference in elevation between the interior floor and the exterior grade, which I would not endorse. In addition, the surrounding grade was neutral and dependent on area drains in hard surfaces that had been cracked by seismic motion, expansive soils, or both, and I suspected that whatever force had cracked them had likely damaged the concealed drains. I disclaim an evaluation of area drains, but I decided to leave a garden hose running in one and quickly discovered that the water backed-up and overflowed several drains. I'd rather identify a problem with something than disclaim it, knowing that grading and drainage problems can lead to a serious lawsuit, and selected a narrative that described the condition and recommended a specialist evaluation and service. Feeling less paranoid, I climbed onto the flat-roofed addition. However, I remained vigilant because every flat roof is suspect until proven perfect and this one wasn't. Water had stood along the leading edge, held by raised edge metal, where mineral stains, recent patches in the capsheet, and daubs of mastic confirmed that the roof had likely leaked. I resolved to inspect the interior walls and ceiling very carefully and to recommend a specialist evaluation regardless of what I might find inside, but a mystery remained. A turbine vent at the center of the addition was turning gently in the early morning breeze and illogically venting the interior space. I stood pondering its existence. What possible use could it have other than as a flue for an avid smoker and pictured a retired seafarer seated at a table in the center of the room, puffing contentedly on a cherry wood pipe as blue smoke curled slowly up and out through the turbine vent, together with the conditioned air.

By the time I'd finished evaluating the roof the buyer's agent arrived, whose smiling face I'd seen on television and numerous billboards. She welcomed me inside, while acknowledging that the flat roof had indeed leaked and been "professionally repaired," and that the house itself had been totally renovated and was now "better than new." I didn't tell her what I thought, but I did wonder what so-called professional would repair a flat roof over living space with daubs of mastic and leave a turbine vent in the middle of it. Regardless, I've made a practice of not sharing information without my clients being present, but when the agent informed me that the clients would not be coming to the inspection because they were entirely satisfied with the renovation and had accepted the house in its "as-is" condition my lawsuit alarm began to sound. A cursory glance confirmed that the interior had been cosmetically renovated, and I wondered what deficiencies the new paint-job and carpets concealed. Nevertheless, I told her that the property had some deficiencies that would be detailed in my report. Her once warm and bubbly demeanor turned frosty, and persisted until the tardy seller's agent arrived. As I conducted my inspection, they whispered to each other and cast furtive glances in my direction, but I ignored them. Interestingly, before the seller's agent left for what she announced was another appointment, I purposefully asked her a few pointed questions about the house, which she seemed reluctant or unwilling to answer, but she did admit that the sellers had never lived in the house, had purchased it with the intention of renovating it for resale, and were selling it "as is." Of course, this absolved them from disclosing anything about its history and left me holding the body, to borrow an old cliché. Regardless, my inspection revealed several other potentially litigious issues, not the least of which was the fact that the family room addition was probably built without permit, and that the additional square footage rendered the vintage heating and air-conditioning system inadequate. I learned later that the listing agent was directly related to the sellers, and that there'd been a prior inspection she'd failed to disclose. That would be enough to make any inspector paranoid. However, I'm not paranoid, and never have been, but I've come under fire before and been hit a couple of times, and there are many people--including attorneys and expert witnesses who just don't seem to give a tinker's damn about anything except money. So, don't wait to be attacked before you raise your prices, because when you're attacked it's going to cost you one way or another. Besides, given the responsibilities that inspectors are willing to accept, they deserve to make at least what the average attorney makes and more. And, remember, money is not the root of all evil it's simply a counter by which culture is distributed.

Grading and Drainage
Grading and drainage is the most important thing that inspectors need to be concerned about, and the first question they should ask themselves when they arrive on-site is: "Where's the water going to go if it rains for forty days and forty nights?" Grading and drainage and moisture related problems, including with roofs, are the leading cause of real estate litigation, and usually result in the most costly lawsuits. To make matters worse, wherever water flows or drips and gathers mold will often follow. I'll comment briefly on mold, and discuss it at greater length later. Mold has been around since the beginning of recorded time and is essential to the life process. Most of it is relatively benign and its threat to humans has been greatly exaggerated in the media, for reasons of publicity and to garner ratings. Fear sells, which has been a great asset to some attorneys and publicity seekers. But Dr. Ronald E. Gots, who has the authority to speak about environmental toxicology, has attempted to set the record straight in his carefully documented article entitled, "Correcting Mold Misinformation," in which he confirms: "Major misinformation has been presented to the public." He goes on to say: "Those groups that benefit most from continued distribution of such misinformation have little scientific or medically credible support for the current level of distress to which they contribute." Regardless of the truth, inspectors should continue to be vigilant. I believe that we have the responsibility to educate our clients, and every report should include information about mold, which in turn should go a long way in helping us to protect ourselves. I even go so far as to recommend air-quality testing and duct cleaning as a prudent investment in environmental hygiene. But let's get back to grading and drainage.

Water is destructive. Without it even expansive soil is powerless. More destruction has probably resulted from water, and particularly in consort with expansive soils, than from most natural disasters. It can flow through fissures in the soil, rise under barometric pressure or capillary action and even find a way through solid surfaces, and few structures are immune to its power. Unless it's provided with a way around a structure it will generally find a way inside, and when it does disputes and litigation are bound to follow. Most building sites are graded in one way or another before a house is built, but few of them are ideal, and moisture intrusion usually remains a possibility. It may take several days of rain or even a flash flood for moisture intrusion to occur, but that rare occurrence wouldn't absolve you of the responsibility of warning your clients about the potential, and if you fail to do so you're likely to be charged with negligence, not breach of contract but negligence, and maybe even fraud. Let me illustrate how this could happen by relating a tale from the trenches that has a happy ending.

Many years ago, I'd finished evaluating a vacant and recently renovated house and found nothing of any consequence to report. The house was situated on a flat and level pad on a lot that for some reason had never been landscaped. There was scrub brush and mustard weed, a narrow concrete pathway leading to the front door, and an equally narrow strip of concrete outside a rear slider, both of which were likely mandated, but no other hard surfaces, no area drains, and no gutters. There were some small shrinkage cracks in the stem walls of the foundation but none of any significant size or structural significance, and the interior floors were three or four inches above the surrounding soil. However, while waiting for my clients, I was glancing through my report, which at the time was comprised of check-sheets with blank portions for written comments, which I'd designed myself and which I printed on-site before learning better. Anyway, the house sat below street level and, although it was in a climate with limited rainfall, I wondered how well the soil might percolate if it had a significant clay, or adobe, content and if area drains weren't installed. I decided to walk around the house once more and reasoned that several inches of water would actually hold against the house in a sunken area of a side yard, and could not only penetrate the tiny cracks in the slab I'd seen earlier but with enough rain could also pass under the sill-plate.

Suddenly concerned, I hurried inside and pulled back the new carpet on the suspect side of the house and found curing cracks contoured by salt-crystals and stained tack-strip with rusted nails, all indisputable proof that moisture had penetrated the interior. Imagine this happening with a house full of furniture. I amended my report to include this observation and recommended an evaluation by a grading and drainage specialist and the installation of drains. Interestingly, I learned later that a neighbor confirmed that the house had indeed flooded a year earlier and then been sold at a discount to a contractor who knew about it but made no attempt to improve conditions on the site while renovating the house. Without that moment of exploration, I might have left myself vulnerable to a serious lawsuit. Don't hesitate to pull back the carpet on an exterior wall. It only takes a moment, and it won't damage anything. You may have noticed that I recommend things that are contrary to industry standards, such as pulling back a carpet. I apologize, but the sad truth is that standards are a last-ditch and probably useless defense that inspector should hope never to need. So, what's the best way to avoid a grading and drainage lawsuit? Inasmuch as inspectors cannot predict the future, the best way that I know is to include a description of an ideal site that prints automatically in every report, and then never endorse a site that doesn't conform to the ideal. This is what prints in each and every one of my reports, which you're welcome to use:

Grading and drainage are the most significant aspects of a property, because of the direct and indirect damage that moisture can have on structures. More damage has resulted from moisture and expansive soils than from most natural disasters, and for this reason we're particularly diligent when evaluating site conditions. In fact, we compare all sites to an ideal. In short, the ideal property will have soils that slope away from the house for a minimum of six feet, and the interior floors will be at least several inches higher than the exterior grade. Also, the residence will have gutters and downspouts that discharge into area drains with catch basins that carry water away to hard surfaces. If a property does not meet this ideal, or if any portion of the interior floor is at or below the exterior grade, we will not endorse it, even though there may be no evidence of moisture intrusion, and recommend that you consult with a grading and drainage contractor. We have discovered evidence of moisture intrusion inside homes when it was raining that would not have been apparent otherwise.

I hope you agree that this statement is entirely reasonable, and that similar statements that educate clients are among the best ways to avoid disputes and lawsuits. But let's not forget about mold. It may not repeat the litigious history of asbestos when attorneys discover that there may not be much money in it, because it's either not covered or continuously disclaimed by inspectors and agents alike. However, you owe it to yourself to include a mold-disclaimer in your report, and to identify any suspect substances that could prove to be mold, and you should always look for it in areas where mold is likely to occur, such as in basements, foundation crawlspaces, around plumbing components and evaporator coils, and in attics with exhaust fans that are not ducted to the exterior. Remember, it is moisture that's the primary threat and not mold. But we'll talk more about this later.

Foundations

The word foundation is a timeless metaphor of strength and stability, and people have natural concerns about the foundations on which their homes are built. For this reason, they need to be educated about foundations in general and specific types in particular, and I include such information in every report. This is what I say about slab-on-grade foundations, and you're also welcome to all or any part of it.

This residence has a bolted, slab foundation. Such foundations are common, but vary considerably from older ones that have no moisture barrier beneath them or reinforcing steel within them to newer ones that have moisture barriers beneath them and adjustable reinforcing steel within them. This type is called a post-tension slab, but it's often impossible to distinguish one type from another in which even the size and spacing of the bolts can vary, although most are concealed. Our inspection of slabs conforms to industry standards. We examine the visible portion of the stem walls on the exterior of the structure for any evidence of significant cracks or structural deformation. However, we do not move furniture or lift carpeting and padding to look for cracks, and we do not use any specialized tools or measuring devices to establish relative elevations or determine any degree of slope or differential settling. Significantly, many slabs are built or move out of level, but the average person would not realize this until there is a difference of more than one inch in twenty feet, which most authorities describe as being tolerable. Interestingly, many slabs are found to contain cracks when the carpet and padding are removed, but there is no absolute standard for evaluating them. However, those that are less than 1/4" and which exhibit no significant vertical or horizontal displacement are not regarded as being structurally threatening. They typically result from common shrinkage, but can also be caused by a deficient mixture of concrete, deterioration through time, seismic activity, adverse soil conditions, and poor drainage, and if they're not sealed they can allow moisture and vapor to enter, and particularly if a residence is surcharged by a hill or a slope, or if downspouts discharge adjacent to the slab. However, in the absence of any major defects, we may not recommend that you consult with a structural engineer or a foundation contractor but this should not deter you from seeking the opinion of any such expert, and for which reason we disclaim any further responsibility.

A similar narrative appears with raised foundations. Such narratives educate clients and sensibly limit liability for inspectors, who are not geo-technical specialists and shouldn't be expected to accept the responsibilities of a specialist. For instance, how many inspectors are aware that American builders continued to use an inferior sand-lime mixture for many years until the development of pressure testing at the turn of the twentieth century proved that Portland cement, which was invented by an Englishman in 1824, was vastly superior to its American counterpart? Was it simply a case of a cultural bias? All foundations are not equal. I've scraped some built at the turn of the twentieth century that had the consistency of a stale crumb cake. This is why informative narratives are essential, and why any foundation defect needs to be documented, and why I favor the use of a report-writer in which endless amounts of information can be stored and entered into a report with a simple click of a mouse. Also, a report-writer can also be used as a reference library in which inspectors can look up information they could not possible hope to remember, but let's consider cracks in slab foundations.

Some inspectors may be inclined to believe that small cracks, which are typically the result of shrinkage, are not worth noting. However, consider the following case involving a house with slab on-grade foundation in a neighborhood with no apparent geological issues, no cracks in the streets, no broken curbs, nothing. The house had been completely renovated, and in perfect condition. It was tastefully furnished, and had a new roof, new windows, new doors, new carpets and tiled floors, to name the major improvements. The only visible defects were cracks in an old and likely original patio slab that could have been due to the absence of expansion joints, the installation of which was not in common practice when the house was built.

It was a house I inspected and written about before, but if you want to read the actual lawsuit, it is case number BC248740, filed in Los Angeles Superior Court on April 16th, 2001. It taught me a lesson that I'll never forget. Approximately one year after my inspection, and in preparation for a major lawsuit between the buyer and the seller, an evaluation by geo-technical experts confirmed that expansive soils were raising and lowering the house as though it were floating on water, which I should have researched and warned my clients about. Doors had moved out of square, and cracks radiated from every opening. The lawsuit revealed that the seller, who happened to be a real estate agent, had acted as his own contractor and failed to disclose he had renovated the house without permits and had concealed an area of broken slab with multiple layers of padding under a carpet. I'd recommended permit research for the remodel, but it was ignored and failed to help me. In truth, the house had appeared to be perfect, and my report included pictures that proved it, and I was shocked by the movement. I had no way of knowing about the concealed layers of padding leveling the slab, and to make matters worse the insurance company elected to settle the case and cancelled my policy, which flew in the face of common sense and made a mockery of justice. Needless to say, every inspector would do well to research soils in specific areas and caution their clients about cracks in hard surfaces. Some cracks in patio slabs, walkways and driveways, are not necessarily a cause for alarm. They result from moderate ground movement, which builders try to accommodate by cutting in expansion joints at every eight feet or so, but inspectors should never make assumptions about such things. They should at least inform their clients about them, and recommend that they seek a second opinion. Every crack is a potential lawsuit, for which reason I always select a narrative that alerts my clients to cracks, such as the following:

There are cracks and/or out-of-square openings in the residence that are indicative of movement, attributable to common settling or seismic activity. However, inasmuch as structures can also move more or less continuously in the presence of expansive soils and we cannot rule this out you should be aware that only a geologist or geo-technical specialist could predict further movement. We can elaborate on this issue, but you should consult with a specialist.

If you feel confident that the cracks you're observing are not particularly significant, you may wish to soften such a narrative or not even use one. Many inspectors believe that less is best and depend on their standards to protect them. I never did, and believe that a detailed report that educates clients affords the best protection. However, this is a difficult decision for any inspector to make, such as whether or not to quote codes. For instance, I commonly find intermediate floor framing that has been insignificantly notched or otherwise modified, and I'm not willing to let go of it because another inspector or contractor may choose to make an issue of something that I considered insignificant, but which would nonetheless leave me liable. So I'll select a narrative such as the following, and leave them with the decision as to what should be done about it:

It's permissible to pierce intermediate floor framing, but the holes should be no larger than one-third of the depth of the material and drilled no closer than two inches from the upper or lower edges. Also, although the framing may be notched, the notch should be no deeper than one-sixth the depth, and never in the middle of the span.

Considering the enormous amount of technical information that inspectors need to be aware of, the specific details in this narrative serve as part of a portable reference library. Some inspectors may not wish to provide such detailed code information, fearing that if they quoted code in one instance that they could be held accountable for other code issues, which inspectors typically disclaim. However, I'm a contractor, and feel that I'm entitled to quote codes if I want to, and like many other inspectors I'm prepared to go beyond industry standards. Nonetheless, inspectors would do well to remember that foundations in seismic areas, together with roofs, grading and drainage, generate more real estate litigation than anything else. The truth is, there is no absolute standard for evaluating cracks and, inasmuch as most are the result of structural movement, each should be identified, described, and recommended for further evaluation and disclaimed.

Vertical cracks in the stem walls of foundations are relatively common, and typically result from shrinkage. Those at the top of the next page were taken from inside a garage and are seismically related, but not everyone agrees on the significance of such cracks. And when money is involved, opinions can range from the rational to the ridiculous.

A veteran foundation contractor, who taught me much of what I know about foundations, paid little attention to such cracks unless there was a significant degree of rotation, but that was in a less litigious era. He would explain how they occur and sometimes pacify his nervous clients by explaining that he'd crawled through an eighteen inch "crack" in the stem wall to evaluate the raised foundation, meaning the screened access of course. However, in today's sue-happy society, nervous clients are best referred to specialists. Nevertheless, there are other issues besides cracks that inspectors need to be concerned about. For instance, if the soils around a foundation extend above the top of the footing and do not slope away for a distance of at least six feet, structural problems could result, as you can see from the picture of a foundation stem wall below that was taken from inside a crawlspace.

In this instance, soils had rested on the stem walls for years and allowed moisture to pass through and deteriorate the concrete, which sloughed off and exposed the rebar, or structural steel, and such a condition could certainly generate a lawsuit.

Shrinkage cracks are common in slab foundations, and are usually small. However, it's possible to find large ones where the slab meets the footing, and which are known as cold-joint separations and result from the footing and slab being poured separately. They're usually not discovered until old carpeting and padding are removed, which commonly happens when a house changes hands, in other words a few weeks or months after it has been inspected. Because of their size, cold-joint separations can seem alarming but they're not structural and are easily sealed with non-shrink grout. However, people have been reported to become hysterical, believing that their house is about to fall down or that the seller had deliberately concealed defects that the inspector should have magically known existed. It's a recurrent nightmare for those inspectors who have tried to convince a disgruntled client that such cracks have little significance. The truth is that all cracks can be said to be structural but not all are structurally alarming, and people really do need to be educated about them no matter how small, in which case their response is likely to be rational instead of hysterical. However, remember that most people are inclined to believe the worst.

I was told about a case in which an inspector had to hire a structural engineer to inform a client about a concealed cold joint separation, but even after being assured by the engineer that the crack had no structural significance the client still decided to sue the inspector in Small Claims Court. Naturally, the inspector paid the engineer to represent him again but in court and fortunately common sense prevailed and the inspector won, or did he? He had to pay the engineer twice, and wasted a day in court when he could have been doing inspections and earning money. True, the judge could have ordered the plaintiff to pay the inspector's costs, but this would have been unusual, and no one should be foolish enough to believe that justice always prevails. For instance, insurance companies are in the business of making money, and if they can spend ten or twenty thousand dollars to settle a lawsuit against an innocent inspector, rather than eighty to a hundred thousand dollars defending an innocent one they will. And the courts are not above awarding a plaintiff a token amount, in order to pacify the litigants on both sides and make the judgment seem equitable. This is clearly unjust, because an inspector's reputation can be discredited, his insurance premiums increased, and a similar claim could result in his policy being cancelled. Unfortunately, that's the price we pay to be inspectors and why report-writers have almost totally replaced check-sheets, and why our tool bags now include specialized instruments.

We shouldn't leave the subject of foundations without talking about sloping floors. Some floors are built out of level, and some are caused by differential settling, or weight bearing down on footings in soil that's inherently unstable, inadequately compacted, or have been destabilized by moisture. Interestingly, builders pay little attention to weight and could only guess at the weight of a house, whereas a shipwright could tell you down to the last pound what a ship weighs. Consequently, houses have a tendency to settle, typically on one side or more or less equally on opposite sides, which leaves the floors crowned in the middle. Although some old-timers still carry marbles to test for sloping floors, they often tend to regard such evidence as being of little consequence. Similarly, many structural engineers agree that one inch of slope in twenty feet is tolerable, and report that differences in elevation are typically not noticed until they exceeds this. However, the trouble with such reasoning is that when attorneys become involved common sense goes out the window, and mercenary experts can always be found who are willing to testify that an inspector was incompetent, or worse, criminally negligent. And now that the majority of inspectors have deep pockets, in the form of errors and omissions insurance, they can no longer rely on the distinction of having common sense. Some states are notoriously more litigious than others, but let me end this topic by acknowledging that I rarely did an inspection without shooting elevations with my laser level, and I certainly wouldn't depend on a contract or a typical industry disclaimer to defend myself. Inspectors willingly accept an enormous responsibility by evaluating properties and, for the most part, for a fraction of the cost that structural engineers, geologists, and other specialists charge, and for this reason alone they should never leave themselves vulnerable to a lawsuit. The golden age of home inspections, in which deals were cinched with a handshake, has past.

Roofs

I've installed a few roofs, and probably inspected thousands, but I'm not an expert by any means, and I'm certainly not qualified to give legal advice. But, for what it's worth, I'll tell you how I attempt to protect myself when inspecting roofs and you can decide what works best for you. But, before we do, let's remember that the truth is not absolute, even though many people believe it to be. First, take a moment to look at the composition shingle roof below.

I took this and other photographs few minutes before a listing agent arrived and saw what I was doing and assured me that the roof had never leaked and had been recently described by a local roofing contractor as "having a few more years of life left." Having viewed the photograph, what do you think? Believe it or not, I actually believe that the agent was repeating what she believed to be the truth, but as far as I was concerned, the roof was beyond its design-life, significantly deteriorated, and could leak, and should be evaluated for replacement by a licensed roofing contractor before the close of escrow, and that's exactly how my report described it.

As strange as it may seem, many people buy houses they've fallen in love with, and like star-crossed lovers they don't want to hear anything negative about it. The average buyer typically wants the answer to four questions: Is the foundation bolted, does the roof leak, will tissue disappear when the toilet is flushed, and is the water pressure good? Of course, they mean water volume and not pressure, but the commonest question that buyers ask inspectors is: "How's the roof?" It's a deceptively simple question that rarely has a simple answer, but it shows the concern that people have about roofs. They want to hear that it doesn't leak, and truly believe that an inspector should be able to guarantee that it won't. And if it leaks after they move in, an inspector is very likely to hear about it from them or their attorney. So the first thing that I try to do is to educate my clients about roofs, and explain to them why I cannot guarantee that a roof won't leak. I never have to think about doing this, because a narrative in my report-writer prints as part of my roof evaluation. Here's the one that I use, and you're welcome to use all or any part of it as long as you do so at your own risk:

There are many different roof types, and every roof will wear differently relative to its age, the number of its layers, the quality of its material, the method of its application, its exposure to direct sunlight or other prevalent weather conditions, and its maintenance. However, regardless of its design-life, every roof is only as good as the waterproof membrane beneath it, which is concealed and cannot be examined without removing the roofing material, and this is equally true of almost all roofs. In fact, the material on most pitched roofs is not designed to be waterproof only water-resistant. There are two basic roof types, pitched and flat. Pitched roofs are the most common, and the most dependable. They are variously pitched, and typically finished with composition shingles that have a design life of twenty to twenty-five years, or concrete, composite, Spanish, or metal tiles that have a design-life of forty to fifty years, and gravel roofs that have a lesser pitch and a shorter design-life of fifteen to twenty years. These roofs may be layered, or have one roof installed over another, which is a common practice but one that is never recommended because it reduces the design-life of the new roof by several years and requires a periodical service of the flashings. These are serviced with mastic, which eventually shrinks and cracks and provides a common point of leakage. However, among the pitched roofs, gravel ones are the least dependable, because the low pitch and the gravel prevent them from draining as rapidly as other roofs. For this reason, they must be conscientiously maintained. In this respect, the least dependable of all roofs are the flat ones, which are also called built-up roofs. Some flat roofs are adequately sloped toward drains but many are not, and water simply ponds and will only be dispersed by evaporation. However, the most common cause of leakage results when roofs are not serviced or kept clean, and foliage and other debris block the drainage channels.

What remains true of all roofs is that it's virtually impossible for anyone to detect a leak except as it's occurring or by specific water tests, which are beyond the scope of our service. Even water stains on walls and ceilings, or on the framing within attics, will not necessarily confirm an active leak without corroborative evidence, which of course can be deliberately concealed. Consequently, only the installer can credibly guaranty that a roof will not leak, and they do. We cannot, and do not give any such guaranty. We evaluate every roof and even attempt to approximate its age, but we will not predict is remaining life expectancy, nor guarantee that it won't leak. Naturally, the sellers or the occupants of a residence generally have the most intimate knowledge of the roof and of its history. Therefore, we recommend that you ask the sellers about it, and that you either include comprehensive roof coverage in your home insurance policy or have an evaluation and roof certification from a local roofing company.

Such narratives not only educate clients they also define the parameters of the inspection, but they're of limited value without another that describes a specific roof. I could have chosen a narrative for any roof type, but here's the one that I use when evaluating a composition shingle roof, which you're also welcome to use with the same caveat:

There are a wide variety of composition shingle roofs, which are comprised of asphalt or fiberglass materials impregnated with mineral granules that are designed to deflect the deteriorating ultra-violet rays of the sun. These roofs are warranted by the manufacturer to last from twenty to twenty-five years, and are typically guaranteed against leaks by the installer for three years. The actual life of the roof will vary, depending on a number of interrelated factors besides the quality of the material and the method of installation. Poor maintenance is the most common cause of roof failure, but a southern exposure can cause a roof to deteriorate prematurely, as will the practice of layering over another roof. However, the first indication of significant wear is when the granules begin to separate and leave pockmarks or dark spots. This is referred to as primary decomposition, which means that the roof is in decline, and therefore susceptible to leakage. This typically begins with the hip and ridge shingles and to the field shingles on the south facing side. This does not mean that the roof is ready to be replaced, but that it should be serviced or monitored. Regular maintenance will certainly extend the life of any roof, and will usually avert most leaks that only become evident after they've caused other damage. This is important, because in accordance with industry standards our inspection service does not include a guaranty against leaks. For such a guaranty, you would need to have a roofing company perform a water test and issue a roof certification. However, the sellers or the occupants will generally have the most intimate knowledge of the roof, and you ask them about its history and then schedule a regular maintenance service.

You'll notice that the disclaimer about not being able to predict roof leaks is repeated. That's intentional, because sometimes it's worth repeating things for greater emphasis. And, of course, there are times when there simply isn't any evidence that a roof might leak, and clients need to understand this so that they won't hold their inspector responsible. I emphasize this, because leaking roofs and poor communication inevitably lead to disputes and lawsuits. I'll explain this further by relating an actual case. I vividly remember looking at blown-up pictures of plaster damage inside a house, which had resulted from a leak in a concrete tile roof that had been inspected a little more than a year earlier and which had no visible defects. What the inspector did not find out until he was actually in Small Claims Court was that the real estate agent represented the buyers as well as the sellers, and who happened to be a close friend of the sellers, had paid to have plaster damage repaired and painted after they'd moved out of state. Fortunately for the inspector, a roofing contractor conceded to the judge that not even a roofing specialist could have predicted such a leak, and that only after viewing new stains inside the house was he able to determine its cause by lifting tiles in a specific area and discovering a split membrane. The out-of-state seller never even responded to the summons, and the inspector and the real estate agent were both absolved of any responsibility. But, if justice had truly prevailed, the dishonest agent would have been held responsible, but for reasons known only to the judge she wasn't. I'm reminded of the wisdom in another ancient aphorism: "A judge decides for ten reasons, nine of which nobody knows." To be sure, justice is an ideal and inspectors would do well to keep this in mind. However, the judgment could have just as easily gone against the inspector, and the trick is to do as much as you can to avoid a similar lawsuit by completing a competent roof inspection and presenting an educational disclaimer.

Before we talk about inspecting roofs, let's first acknowledge that inspecting them can be dangerous, and that personal safety should be the primary concern of every inspector. I liked to walk on roofs whenever possible, but if they were too high, or too steep, or too slippery I always reminded myself that my inspection fee was not equal to the risk. However, some roofing material shouldn't be walked on, such as Spanish tile, some composite tile, and some metal and concrete tiles. I learned this many years ago in the company of a veteran inspector who was training me. He was a hefty fellow and was making his way down a concrete tile roof while shouting observations for me to write: "There are six broken tiles," he shouted. Then I heard a distinct crunch. "Make that seven," he continued. There was a louder crunch and then another as he neared the edge. "There are eight broken tiles; there are nine broken tiles," he growled without missing a beat, but I was doubled over in laughter and couldn't write anything. When I'm unable or unwilling to walk a roof, I select a narrative from my library that explains why and confirms that I inspected it from a variety of vantage points, such as from the ground, with or without binoculars, from the top a ladder, from overlooking windows, and from within the attic, after which I add whatever evaluation or recommendation for service is appropriate. Now, let's talk about roofing materials.

There are a wide variety of roofing materials, some better than others, so you need to be familiar with the type and resiliency of the materials prevalent in your area, as well as the manufacturer's guaranty and the more limited installer's warranty. I like to look at every square foot of a roof, and as much of it as I can see from within an attic where stains from leaks or stress to the rafters and sheathing might be apparent. A single water stain below any roof other than a wood roof on spaced-sheathing is enough for me to recommend a specialist evaluation. But, before we continue with a discussion of other components, let's talk about layering. Layering may be common practice, but it's never sensibly recommended. However, it's not always obvious. I know of a case in which an inspector was sued over a roof on his first independent inspection. Perched at the top of his ladder, he had lifted the shingles at the edge of a roof and seen only one layer and the felt underlayment, which he indicated in his check-sheet report. Shortly after escrow closed and when the new owner was in the process of adding an addition, it was discovered that the roof had three layers, which a City building inspector insisted had to be removed before the addition could be tied into it. The inspector was subsequently sued in Small Claims Court and lost. What he'd failed to realize was that the roof had been indexed, or that successive layers of shingle had been cut back to a point above the top-plate. The plaintiff successfully argued that the inspector should have noticed what a more skilled inspector would have, which was that the toes of the roof jacks were not exposed and that a telltale hump above the plate-line extending the length of the roof confirmed that the roof had been layered and indexed. This is worth remembering when you're evaluating composition shingle roofs on houses that are twenty-five years or older and not likely to be original.

Many roofing materials are similar but they're not equal, and their design-life can range from twenty to fifty years. Therefore, the first thing that I do is to try to estimate the age of a roof. This is not always possible, but if you know the age of the house it's not difficult and is likely to be among the first questions your clients ask. Just make sure that your estimate of its age is given as an estimate and not as a statement of fact, and never predict how long a roof is likely to last. One veteran inspector made the mistake of stating in his report that his clients "should budget for a new roof," which they later argued led them to believe that the roof had several more years of life left, which was contrary to what a roofing contractor told them after escrow closed, so they sued him in Small Claims Court. The judge was sympathetic, but rendered the opinion that the inspector should have recommended a second opinion because the roof was old, and ordered him to pay the plaintiff three thousand dollars in partial compensation for the cost a new roof. Language is subject to interpretation; so make sure that your narratives consist of statements of indisputable facts. Sellers and agents alike are infamous for telling inspectors that a roof doesn't leak. Yet few of them have actually walked a roof or crawled inside an attic when it was raining to see if there are any drips being soaked up by insulation, and I wonder how many of them would be willing to testify in defense of an inspector? Remember, telling a client to obtain an installation permit to confirm the age of a roof is entirely reasonable, and a detailed report confirms a thorough evaluation. Besides, a recommendation for service could prevent a lawsuit. For this reason, I rarely leave a roof without having discovered something that needs to be serviced. This is important, because I have a clause in my contract that my clients are required to initial in which they agree to hold me harmless for any alleged defect involving a component or condition I've recommended for service or a second opinion. And, in truth, most of the roofs that I inspected did need service. Roof leaks usually result as a consequence of poor maintenance and neglect, which is why built-up, or flat, roofs are humorously but intelligently described as being "designed to leak," and that's a fact. I spend much more time inspecting flat roofs than any other type, and almost as much time inspecting roof drainage, and I always include a narrative that explains why they need to be maintained and why I won't endorse any that are not relatively new or perfect in all respects.

Penetrations and intersecting roof planes are sealed with flashings. Most are made of metal, but some are formed with mastic and roofing material. I have read two inspection reports of the same roof that were as different as chalk and cheese; one was brief and described a composition shingle roof as being newer and in good condition, which was true. The second and more recent report was far more detailed, and described the roof installation as being inferior due to the absence of metal valley flashings. The most recent report was commissioned by an attorney who hoped to add to a list of petty complaints designed to discredit an inspector, and he found an expert witness willing to help him do so. The valleys were not sealed with metal flashings but they were laced, which is an old and respected method of sealing a valley and the mark of a craftsman, but this was never pointed out by anyone or acknowledged by the so-called expert. The inspector's insurance company elected to settle the case, rather than defend him. Unfortunately, the lawsuit cost him his deductible and made him realize what many inspectors have come to realize that justice does not always prevail. He was already a competent inspector, but the experience made him a more cautious one, and convinced him to abandon his word-document reports for a report-writer that he could improve with use. The last word on roof penetrations must be given to skylights, and there's really not much to say about them except that, like flat roofs, they commonly leak. So, if you were to look through the narratives in my libraries about skylights, you'd find that all of them include some form of the verb "to leak."

Water is a mighty force that has to be respected. So make sure that the roof you're inspecting has a good pitch and drains rapidly and directly, or be prepared to warn your clients about what are called design-flaws or points at which water has to change direction to leave a roof, as well as any other impediment to drainage. Then, make sure that your roof evaluation is detailed and includes rational disclaimers where appropriate. Even when there are no deficiencies on a roof, I always describe the way in which penetrations or intersecting roof surfaces are sealed, and recommend that they be inspected annually, and that the drainage system be cleaned and inspected seasonally. Too many competent inspectors have been sued because they lacked communication skills, and were trapped in the web of words that attorneys spin. Too late, inspectors learn of expensive carpets, exotic furniture and family heirlooms that have been allegedly damaged beyond repair and of families who've been financially and emotionally devastated, and who can only be made whole again with the magic elixir of money.

Chimneys

The word chimney is actually a misnomer that has come to include every part from the crown to the footing, and everything else in between. However, there are two basic types of chimneys, metal and masonry ones that are built on-site, brick by brick, assembled on-site with prefabricated components, or pre-cast in factories and trucked to a site and raised as finished structures. Chimneys are primarily heating systems that sustain the combustion process and the release of heat. Their use, and certainly the inspection of them, involves a certain degree of risk relative to their type, age, and use in the climate in which they function. For instance, an old, coal-burning, single-walled, brick chimney on the east coast is far more suspect than a similar chimney on the West coast that's venting ornamental gas-logs. Regardless, chimneys are complicated and feature prominently in lawsuits. For this reason, I include an educational narrative with every chimney that I inspect. I don't regard the narrative that follows as being the best possible, but if you don't have a better one you're certainly welcome to it and any others that appear in this book for that matter. My report-writer library actually includes more than eighteen thousand industry-standard narratives that I'm constantly polishing or revising in one way or another, in order to better educate clients and shield inspectors from the ever-present threat of lawsuits. However, this is what is included in my reports about chimneys in general:

There are a wide variety of chimneys, which represent an even wider variety of interrelated components that comprise them. However, there are three basic types: single-walled metal, masonry, and pre-fabricated metal ones that are commonly referred to as factory-built. Single-walled metal ones should not be confused with factory-built ones, and are rarely found in residential use, but masonry and factory-built ones are in common use. Our inspection of them is that of a generalist, not a specialist, and meets industry standards. However, significant areas of chimney flues cannot be adequately viewed during a field inspection, as has been documented by the Chimney Safety Institute of America, which reported in 1992: "The inner reaches of a flue are relatively inaccessible, and it should not be expected that the distant oblique view from the top or bottom is adequate to fully document damage even with a strong light." Therefore, because our inspection of chimneys is limited to those areas that can be viewed without dismantling any portion of them, and does not include the use of specialized equipment, we will not guaranty their integrity and recommend that they be evaluated by a specialist in accordance with NFPA standards before the close of escrow.

Such narratives are essential to any report, and although most clients shouldn't need to be told that there are parts of a chimney that cannot be seen with the naked eye, it doesn't hurt to remind them and any potential attorney. However, the real problem with disclaimers is that they can leave inspectors with a false sense of security and prevent them from doing a conscientious inspection. Besides, a disclaimer is no defense against a charge of negligence. Therefore, inspectors should decide in advance which chimneys represent a threat and are worthy of a careful evaluation, so that a disclaimer does not also become a trap. For instance, just because inspectors might disclaim an evaluation of a flue because portions of it are not visible, it should not stop them from getting their heads and shoulders inside a fireplace to get the best possible view of the smoke shelf and throat. I'll illustrate this by telling you about a chimney that I inspected a few years ago in a very expensive and completely remodeled house.

Viewed from the roof, there was nothing unusual about the chimney. It met the 3-2-10 drafting rule, included a cricket and tight flashings, had terra-cotta liners, and a spark arrestor-weather cap combination, which I removed and had a perfect view of most of the liners, which were not even carbon-stained, and the hearth and its surround appeared to be new, as you can see in the first picture. I didn't get my head and shoulders inside the fireplace, because I was satisfied with everything I'd seen, and was reluctant to move the objects on the hearth and risk dropping and breaking one. Besides, the back and sidewalls were pristine and the log-starter not only responded but included an ornate, brass-plated key. Someone had obviously spent a lot of money on the renovation. Anyway, just as I was about to move on with the inspection, I imagined hearing the voice of an attorney: "Tell me, Sir, did you even attempt to look at the smoke shelf?" I hesitated, and then imagined hearing the voice of my wife: "Well, did you?"

Suddenly motivated, I removed objects from the hearth, slid my head and shoulders inside the firebox, and saw what you see in the second picture, exposed wood and an opening adjacent to the lintel large enough to qualify as an attic access. The first fire in this fireplace could have been the last, because it would have likely burned the house down. Later, I showed the picture to my wife and basked in her praise, knowing that even a schoolboy could have identified such a mind-boggling fire-hazard. Oh, the power of paranoia and the voice of my lovely wife.

Needless to say, every chimney should be examined carefully. The old cast-iron chimneys that remain in use today are rare, and found mostly in rural areas. They can get hot enough to burn the skin and are a safety-hazard, and inspectors should disclaim them unless they're familiar with them and the ordinances governing their use. Even then, I would include a cautionary narrative that warns clients about the dangers they pose. By contrast, modern prefabricated chimneys are among the safest but they have a more limited design life and are not always assembled with all of the factory-approved components. In fact, they generate a disproportionate number of disputes. Interestingly, many of the defects that I've seen were readily apparent without dismantling any portion of them. One that I inspected was missing the transition between the firebox and the flue, and it was plain enough to see. In spite of this, the chimney had been signed off five years earlier when it was installed, and before the drywall was installed and the firebox and flue were exposed and visible. Furthermore, I was told that it had also been approved by an inspector who'd inspected the house and who still remained liable under a four-year statute of limitation. Realizing that our standards of practice don't guaranty

the protection they should, I often go beyond them. For instance, not too long ago, while inspecting another chimney, I realized that I could get an uninterrupted view of its flue if I removed the cap. So, I did, and this is what I saw. You can see what appears to be a homemade plastic damper to prevent energy loss I suppose, but you're probably wondering what was inside the plastic damper where no one would think to look; was it shredded pieces of newspaper or hundreds of dollars in unmarked bills? I'll never tell, but the chimney will draft better after my free service of removing the plastic bag.

Masonry chimneys are even more suspect. There are three basic types: one that's lined one that's unlined, and a third that's pre-cast in a factory, trucked to a site and erected. Obviously, regional concerns dictate which chimney is best. In earthquake country, people would prefer not to have an exterior two-story masonry chimney towering above them, or a single-brick one for that matter. And in regions where fossil fuels are burned continuously, one would rather have a lined flue to resist the effects of corrosive gases. However, before we elaborate on the distinction between lined and unlined chimneys, we should consider the pre-cast ones, which are also referred to as a tilt-ups, and which I describe in a narrative to my clients, as follows and which you're welcome to use:

Pre-cast concrete chimneys are built in factories and then trucked to a building site and erected, as distinct from masonry chimneys that are built on site with individual bricks and mortar. In this respect, pre-cast chimneys are unique. However, like other masonry chimneys they're vulnerable to seismic activity, but unlike masonry chimneys they're also subject to cracks that are induced by the interaction of moisture and a chemical additive called calcium chloride to speed the curing process that causes the reinforcing steel within the chimney to expand and crack the chimney wall. Such cracks may be small, but they're nonetheless subject to stringent repairs stipulated by the manufacturer. However, if any crack penetrates the chimney wall it cannot be repaired and the chimney must be removed. For this reason, we recommend that all pre-cast chimneys be video-scanned or certified by a specialist familiar with them before the close of escrow.

This narrative is self-explanatory, so we can move on to a discussion of the inspection process, which typically begins on the outside. Based on the age of the residence, you should have an idea of how old a chimney is, which could affect your evaluation of it. However, you should identify it as being interior or exterior, single-story, two-story, or multi-level, metal or masonry, lined or unlined, so that you can select a descriptive narrative from your report-writer to include with your evaluation of its components. Next, you should look for cracks in the walls or bent flashings that confirm movement or structural damage. Then you should examine it from the roof's surface. The first thing that you want to confirm is that it meets the 3-2-10 rule used to predict drafting, which states that in order to draft well a chimney should extend at least three feet above a roof, and two feet above any point measured in a ten foot radius. If the chimney is an exterior type, you may wish to test it for movement by rocking it gently. Strength is not a factor in this regard, and you should exercise extreme caution. Exterior masonry chimneys will permit some movement, but you should be able to decide what seems normal and what seems excessive, or what's commonly described as a hinge-effect, and decide whether such movement is being permitted by a structural break at the roofline or further down at the shoulder, and report it as such. It's also important to examine the chimney walls for cracks or washed-out mortar joints. Reporting on something as simple as washed-out mortar joints is important and especially if there's nothing else to report, because it confirms that a chimney was examined carefully enough to make a detailed observation. Although not exposed to weather, the chimney walls inside an attic should also be examined carefully. Chimneys are structurally independent, and there should be two inches of airspace between an interior chimney and any combustibles, and one inch of airspace on exterior ones. Now, let's consider some of the common components.

The mortared crowns on masonry chimneys are shaped to shed water and prevent erosion. They should be examined to ensure that they'll perform well, and if cracked or damaged should be recommended for service. Weather caps and spark-arrestors need no explanation. I always attempt to remove them to get a better look at the flue, or I report that I was unable to so. However, for aesthetic reasons, some builders elect to enclose the cap of prefabricated chimneys with a decorative shroud that may not be part of the installation package. These shrouds can inhibit drafting and convectional cooling, which is essential for performance and should be removed if not factory-approved. Regardless of the chimney type, the liner is the most critical component. Lined chimneys are the most dependable, whereas unlined and single-walled chimneys are suspect. In fact, The Chimney Safety Institute of America states: "all unlined chimneys, irrespective of the fuel used, are very liable to become defective through disintegration of the mortar joints," and this is equally true of the mortar used to coat the walls of unlined flues. However, this is not a reason to condemn all unlined chimneys. Those in warmer climates that are in good condition and are used either infrequently or to vent ornamental gas-logs should not be categorically condemned. Regardless, inspectors are ethically obligated to report everything that they know about a particular chimney type, if only to safeguard their clients from dishonest people who might try to take advantage of them. Interestingly, more and more inspectors are recommending a specialist evaluation in accordance with NFPA 212 standards on the transfer of a property, and I certainly did but I still evaluated them. Some real estate agents don't appreciate such information, and typically dismiss it as being boiler-plate, when it's essential information that confirms an inspector's professionalism.

They are different types of flue liners, but the most common are made of metal or vitreous clay. All liners provide a vent to the exterior and a thermal barrier that protects the surrounding walls from corrosive gases. Although the flues of unlined chimneys are commonly plastered with mortar, which is intended to have the same effect as a liner, it is generally agreed that mortar is a poor substitute. Significantly, flue failures are the most common cause of chimney fires, but liners that were either installed incorrectly, degraded by weather, seismic activity, or thermal extremes have also contributed to such failures, and it's essential to examine them carefully. Damage can be apparent in two forms, either as a loss of material, referred to as spalling, or as longitudinal cracks. Both typically result from moisture contamination, the stress induced by thermal extremes or both, which could predicate a chimney fire and should be reported. Cracks in liners might appear to be small and insignificant, but they enlarge and vent flammable gases when a fire is raging. I've seen a video conducted under controlled conditions of flue cracks expanding that were astonishing and utterly convincing.

Damage or separations to factory-built flues can be equally dangerous, and are capable of drafting flames and volatile gases. Such damage could be apparent from within the attic where the metal flue may be exposed. However, chimneys installed in many jurisdictions since 1992 are required to have their flues enclosed in a drywall chase. Nevertheless, if the flue is exposed, examine it carefully, and make sure that each section is securely attached and supported and that fire-block surrounds it on the attic floor to isolate it from the oxygen-rich atmosphere of an attic. The best possible view of a flue, other than from the top down, is from within a fireplace. You'll need a strong flashlight, and be able to position your head and shoulders inside the fireplace. However, before you wiggle inside and look up, test the damper to make sure that it's functional and releases anything that might be behind it, such as soot, twigs, and the occasional dead rodent, reptile, or bird. When you do look up, you should confirm that there's a smooth transition between the firebox and the flue, and that there are no gaps between the flue and the chimney wall that could allow flames or combustible gases to penetrate. If angles or anything else obstruct your view of the entire flue, you should make sure that your report indicates this and that you disclaim an evaluation of it. However, before moving on to a discussion of other components it would be worthwhile to mention the by-products of combustion common to chimneys. These by-products are usually grouped under the common term creosote, the nature of which is still not fully understood despite advances in chemical knowledge. Regardless, disputes over chimneys commonly start when a client calls in a specialist to have a flue cleaned. Some of these so-called specialists take the opportunity to sell people components or services that they may not need, by alarming them first about the threat of a chimney fire. And inspectors can never hope to prevail against the testimony of a specialist, and must protect themselves as best they can with sensible disclaimers, such as the following, which I include with every chimney evaluation:

Chimney flues need to be cleaned periodically, to prevent the possibility of chimney fires. However, the complex variety of deposits that form within chimney flues as a result of incomplete combustion, and that contribute to such fires, are complicated and not easily understood. They range from soot, or pure carbon, that does not burn, to tars that can ignite. All of these deposits are commonly described as creosote, but creosote has many forms, ranging from crusty carbon deposits that can be easily brushed away, to tar-glazed creosote that requires chemical cleaning. These deposits need to be identified and treated by a specialist. However, cleaning a chimney is not a guaranty against a fire. Studies have proven that a significant percentage of chimney fires have resulted within one month of a chimney being cleaned, and many more have resulted within a six-month period.

Some forms of creosote actually confirm that a chimney fire has occurred. The resulting deposits often look like expanded tar bubbles, foamy or sponge-like deposits, and thin, flaky wafers that collapse at a touch. However, they reduce the diameter of a flue and impede drafting and convectional cooling, and whenever you see any deposits you should recommend that the chimney be evaluated for service by a specialist. I actually take a few extra minutes to interpret carbon deposits within a firebox to see what they might teach me. However, the evidence of a chimney fire is not always apparent, but a detailed inspection and observation is essential.

 A chimney has its own foundation, a firebox or combustion chamber with an ash-pit, a smoke chamber that provides a mitered transition into a flue, a hearth, and a surround, and possibly a mantle. The firebox is typically lined with refractory brick or prefabricated metal or terra cotta panels that contain the combustion process. Soot or carbon deposits surrounding the firebox could confirm that the chimney does not draft well, as is obvious in the picture shown below.

However, you should look for other indications that a chimney may not draft well, such as restrictions within the smoke chamber or an inadequate distance between the lintel and the flue. Regardless, any damage to the firebox should be described in detail, such as thermally warped metal panels and loose, cracked, or missing refractory bricks. Cracks in refractory bricks are relatively common, but cracks in the firebox of a pre-cast chimney, and particularly those in the breastplate are serious and should be referred to a specialist. It's not uncommon to see separations contouring the opening, which can literally draft a flame in the same way that a flue does and must be sealed. In fact, every crack or void in a firebox should be described.

For instance, it's common to find a void around the gas pipe in the sidewall of a factory-built chimney that can draft a flame beyond the combustion chamber and should be sealed with thermal caulk. Remember, any breach of the firebox is a safety-hazard, but also remember that you're a generalist and not a specialist. Therefore, report even the slightest defect and never hesitate to recommend a specialist evaluation.

It's important to turn on ornamental logs and log-starters, at least long enough to smell the gas and confirm they're functional. Other than that, there is little else to do except to report on their condition. This brings us to the end of our discussion of chimneys, but a few words of caution for new inspectors. Although I'm willing to endorse any single-story lined chimney in good condition if I have a reasonable view of each liner, I won't endorse any other masonry chimney. My reasons are simple. Firstly, experience has taught me that there are many so-called specialists whether by ignorance or greed fabricate deficiencies and fuel disputes and lawsuits. Secondly, and in accordance with NFPA 211 standards, I recommend a specialist evaluation on the transfer of a property, and that gives me penultimate protection. This is particularly true with clients who'd rather believe the worst, and it is nearly impossible for any inspector to prevail against the testimony of a specialist. However, even if you do happen to prevail in a lawsuit it will still cost you, one way or another. Therefore, smart inspectors will avoid disputes at any cost, and the best way do this is with a conscientious evaluation that includes reasonable disclaimers and detailed observations, and recommendations for specialist evaluations.

Plumbing

I could be wrong, but I don't believe that plumbing features prominently in lawsuits, and certainly not among the more expensive ones, so I'll be brief. Having said that, I believe we have the responsibility to educating our clients and protecting ourselves. To that end, the part of my report that deals with plumbing begins with a narrative that I regard as a first-line of defense and prints automatically. Here it is, and please feel free to take all or any part that you might find useful.

We evaluate plumbing systems and their components in accordance with industry standards, which include testing for pressure and functional flow. Plumbing systems have common components but they are not uniform. In addition to fixtures, components typically consist of gas pipes, potable water pipes, drain and vent pipes, shut-off valves, which we don't test if they're not in daily use, pressure regulators, pressure relief valves, and water-heating devices. The best and most dependable water pipes are copper or plastic, because they're not subject to the build-up of minerals that bond to the inside of galvanized pipes and gradually reduce their inner diameter and the volume of water. A water softener will remove most of these minerals, but not once they're bonded within the pipes, for which there's no other remedy other than a re-pipe. Water pressure is commonly confused with water volume, but whereas high water volume is good high water pressure is not. In fact, whenever the street pressure exceeds eighty pounds per square inch a regulator is recommended, which typically comes factory preset between forty-five and sixty-five pounds per square inch. However, regardless of the pressure, leaks will occur in any system, and particularly in one with older galvanized pipes, and commonly when the regulator fails and high pressure starts to stress the washers and diaphragms within the various components.

In addition to this, my report includes a disclaimer about drainpipes:

We attempt to evaluate drainpipes by flushing every drain that has an active fixture while observing its draw and watching for blockages or slow drains, but this is not a conclusive test and only a video-scan of the main drain and sewer pipe would confirm its actual condition. However, you can be sure that blockages will occur, usually relative in severity to the age of the system, and will range from minor ones in the branch lines, or at the traps beneath sinks, tubs, and showers, to major blockages in the main line. The minor ones are easily cleared, either by chemical means or by removing and cleaning traps. However, if tree roots grow into the sewer pipe, repairs can be expensive and even include replacing it. For these reasons, we recommend that you ask the sellers if they've ever experienced any drainage problems, or you may wish to have the main waste line video-scanned before the close of escrow. Failing this, you should obtain an insurance policy that covers blockages and damage to the main line. However, most policies only cover plumbing repairs within the house, or the cost of rooter service, which are usually relatively inexpensive when compared to the cost of replacing a main sewer pipe.

As I've mentioned, these narratives print automatically and before I've evaluated even a single component. However, as I evaluate them my report-writer gives me the ability to select from a series of shorter but more specific narratives to describe my findings and document my evaluation. For instance, when evaluating a gas water heater, I select a narrative that educates my clients about gas water heaters in general, after which I select one that confirms its location, age, and capacity. Then, I select narratives that comment on individual components: the vent pipe, the pressure-temperature relief valve, the seismic straps, et cetera. However, as with all other components, my library also allows me to select a single generic narrative, with fill-in blanks, that describes the unit in summary. For example, having identified its location, age, and capacity, I could select a narrative that confirms that it has no visible defects. This makes the report shorter, but leaves me more vulnerable to a complaint or lawsuit, so I don't always avail myself of this option. Besides, commenting on each component compels me to look at each in turn. Of course, the total cost of replacing a water heater is affordable to settle a dispute and cheaper than a lawsuit, but let's return to more general plumbing issues.

As I've acknowledged, I really like military metaphors and regard every inspection as a reconnaissance mission into enemy territory. Therefore, the first thing I recommend is trying to anticipate the attack. For instance, you're far more likely to be attacked because of galvanized pipes than copper ones, and particularly if they're old, non-domestic, and pass through an attic. I don't know if this is a national phenomenon, but I've come across Korean galvanized pipes that have a history of premature leaks, and if the pipes pass through an attic and leak you can imagine the damage that could result. On a related issue, I always test and often demonstrate water volume, or functional flow, and then I select one of several narratives that characterize it, all of which begin with the introductory clause: "As I've demonstrated." This clause could prevent someone from claiming later that they either "didn't realize," or "didn't understand," or some such lame excuse for not excepting responsibility and, instead, blaming me. We shouldn't leave the subject of galvanized pipes without mentioning repair-clamps, which are metal with a rubber or neoprene sleeve and commonly found repairing pin-hole leaks on old galvanized pipes. As a convenient and cheap and easy repair, these clamps confirm an amateur or an unprofessional service and finding even one repair-clamp on a galvanized pipe is enough for me to recommend a complete copper re-pipe. This may sound excessive but it's completely reasonable, and if a client chooses to ignore my recommendation, so be it. I'm less likely to receive a complaint when a pipe in the attic bursts and a ceiling collapses on expensive furniture or, worse, on someone asleep in their bed.

The final word about plumbing should be given to a plumbing component that cannot be seen: the main drain and the sewer pipe. It would be interesting to know how many inspectors have had call-backs involving a blockage or back-up, but blockages are common, never pleasant, sometimes very costly to repair, and not covered by most home protection policies. For this reason, I would ask every inspector to forget that the standards of practice disclaim an evaluation of things that cannot be seen. Plain old common sense confirms that we cannot evaluate what we cannot see, but play close attention to what can be seen. I run a lot of water, put drains under pressure, observe the draw at every fixture, and flush toilets twice. But this doesn't mean that I endorse main sewer pipes, because I don't. I take into consideration the age of a residence, which tells me what the sewer pipe is likely made of, I note how far it has to travel to join the public sewer and if there are mature trees in the vicinity, and then I select one of several narratives. And each and every narrative that I select recommends that the main sewer pipe be video-scanned for one reason or another. Here's my parting word of advice on this subject: never submit a report that does not recommend having a main sewer pipe video-scanned or endorsed by the seller or builder. Now we can move on to a subject that demands respect and one that belongs among the great mysteries of nature, electricity.

Electricity

As much as I've tried to completely understand electricity I've failed, and telling what I know about it will make this section brief. I understand that it kills and of that I'm certain, and the fact that I'm still alive seems a miracle indeed, and I'll tell you why. Many years ago, I was removing the interior cover from a sixty or seventy amp Zinsco panel, and in the process I must have inadvertently made contact with the uninsulated feeder bars. Anyway, it shot a lightning bolt of plasma over my shoulder that was awesome, and left me trembling like a leaf in the wind and thanking my lucky stars that I was still standing and alive. I've been told arcing the panel couldn't have killed me, but I don't believe it. Anyway, I promptly called an electrician, paid him to replace the cover and watched, hoping to partake of the mystery. He was a Russian with a strong accent, and waved away my warnings with a disdainful grin. I stood a safe distance from him, and watched meekly as he positioned himself on a wooden board, wearing goggles and special gloves, and looking more regal than a Czar. Then, as he slid the scorched interior cover back inside the panel, a second bolt shot out of the panel and over his shoulder and reminded me twice in one day how sweet it is to be alive. Seriously, I now have an informative narrative that describes the old Zinsco panels and their insane design. I've come a long way since that eventful day, and have tried very hard to overcome my fears and ignorance by learning as much as I can about electricity, but to no avail. In truth, you'd be foolish to believe you could learn a great deal about electricity by listening to what I have to say, but this much I've learned.

First of all, I depend on a pre-selected narrative that prints with every report. Of course, you're welcome to use it or any part of it but at your own risk.

There are a wide variety of electrical systems with an even wider variety of components, and one particular system may not conform to current standards or provide the same degree of service and safety. What is most significant about electrical systems is that the National Electrical Code [NEC] is not retroactive, and therefore many residential systems do not comply with the latest safety standards. Regardless, we are not electricians and in compliance with our standards of practice we only test a representative number of switches and outlets and do not perform load-calculations to determine if the supply meets the demand. However, in the interests of safety, we regard every electrical deficiency and recommended upgrade as a latent hazard that should be serviced as soon as possible, and that the entire system be evaluated and certified as safe by an electrician. Therefore, it's essential that any recommendations that we may make for service, a second opinion, or upgrades should be completed before the close of escrow, because an electrician could reveal additional deficiencies or recommend upgrades for which we would disclaim any further responsibility. However, we typically recommend upgrading outlets to have ground fault protection, which is a relatively inexpensive but essential safety feature. These outlets are often referred to as GFCI's, or ground fault circuit interrupters and, generally speaking, have been required in specific locations for more than thirty years, beginning with swimming pools and exterior outlets in 1971, and the list has been added to ever since: bathrooms in 1975, garages in 1978, spas and hot tubs in 1981, hydro tubs, massage equipment, boat houses, kitchens, and unfinished basements in 1987, crawlspaces in 1990, wet bars in 1993, and all kitchen countertop outlets with the exception of refrigerator and freezer outlets since 1996. Similarly, AFCI's or arc fault circuit interrupters, represent the latest in circuit breaker technology, and have been required in new construction for bedrooms since 2002. However, inasmuch as arc faults cause thousands of electrical fires and hundreds of deaths each year, we also recommend installing them as a prudent safety feature.

I make a conscientious effort to evaluate every component, beginning with the overhead service conductor and the main panel. If I haven't already made the point about personal safety, I'll emphasize it now. Don't touch any panel without first testing it for errant electricity with a tic-tester or similar instrument, or by placing the back of your right hand close to the panel, which would make the small hairs on the back of your hand bristle if the cover is energized. However, if you did accidentally touch it your fingers would curl away from the cover and the current would likely flash to ground down the right side of your body and not damage the delicate cardiac tissue on your left side. As to amperage, size does matter when it comes to electricity. So identify the manufacturer of the panel and its age, note its size, confirm that its circuits are clearly labeled, determine that the breakers and wire sizes match, make sure there's no single-strand aluminum wire in use for anything other than a ground, and confirm that the panel is grounded, preferably double-grounded. It only takes one deficiency for me to recommend a licensed electrician, even if I find something as commonplace as circuits that are not labeled.

I'm confident that most of you know about suspect panels, such as Zinsco Sylvania and Federal Pacific with Stablok breakers, but you should be equally wary of any panel that's old or small. Any unidentified single-strand aluminum wiring could certainly generate a lawsuit, because it is costly to retrofit with hermetically sealed connections at every terminal, known as "copalum crimps." On a less serious note, recommended upgrades can become contentious. For instance, although most inspectors recommend upgrades, many also try to keep realtors happy and point out that a residence is not required to meet the latest National Electrical Code, which isn't retroactive, but as you can see from my general disclaimer I regard every upgrade as absolutely essential. If a residence doesn't have grounded outlets and ground fault protected ones it should be upgraded, and remember that arc-fault breakers that protect bedroom circuits were introduced in 2002. All inspectors have to do is to keep reminding themselves that electricity kills. In my limited and mostly private experience, I've learned of three deaths by electrocution, one was the death of a handyman and involved a panel I'd inspected and recommended immediate service, which was a hopeless tangle of wires concealing serious defects. The second death was an electrician's apprentice, who was working on a miswired exhaust fan while stretched out in an attic on foil-faced insulation, and the third also happened in an attic and apparently had something to do with reversed polarity and a housekeeper turning on a bedroom light switch, or so I heard. I was not given any lurid details, or interested in hearing them.

Heating and Air-conditioning

Inspectors are self-reliant and willing to accept the responsibility of evaluating most of the complicated components that make up a house, and usually for a mere percentage of the fee that most professionals charge for evaluating a single thing. In the good old days, inspectors used to report that a system was or wasn't working, but the times have changed and inspectors are being progressively threatened by lawsuits and heating and air-conditioning are featuring prominently. The reasons for this are understandable. Without adequate heat, a house is not a home. In fact, without heat it's not a habitable dwelling, and without air-conditioning the sweltering heat of summer can turn ordinary people into spiteful tyrants, but it took me awhile to learn this. I fact, after having completed thousands of inspections it dawned on me that most of the complaints and threatened lawsuits I'd heard about had to do with heating and air-conditioning. After thinking about this, I also realized that some of the nuisance calls I'd had to deal with could have been avoided if I'd provided my clients with more detailed information about how systems works, how they should be maintained, and even what to expect in the way of problems, not the least of which would have been to warn them about the crooked contractors who'd say almost anything to make money. Regardless, let's consider some contentious and potentially litigious issue with heating and air-conditioning.

The first thing I check for with heating and air-conditioning is the age of the components. The older they are, the more suspect they are. This is particularly true of combustion chambers, an evaluation of which is disclaimed in industry standards, but which are contemptuously dismissed by attorneys as "boiler-plate." Besides, industry standards can make inspectors lazy and give them a false sense of security. You'd be surprised at how many inspectors have been sued over cracked fireboxes and how meaningless their disclaimers were, simply because they weren't sued for breach of contract but for negligence. In fact, for many years, I rarely gave combustion chambers anything more than a casual thought. Then, I began to do more conscientious evaluations that included removing flame covers. The first time I did this I had a view of a combustion chamber I'd never seen before, and to my delight I saw a distinct crack at the fluted top of one of the chambers. Suddenly, I was a hero. My clients were virtually guaranteed a new furnace, and the wicked witch of the west representing the sellers wasn't able to argue with me. From that point on, the inner recesses of combustion chambers that were once a mystery became more and more familiar, and I was occasionally able to confirm cracks. Even when they weren't cracked, I was able to select a narrative from my report-writer that accurately described the visible portions as being in reasonable condition, thermally fatigued, rust-contaminated by condensation, or simply beyond design-life and worthy of a second opinion. And combustion chambers are rarely perfect, which allow me to sensibly recommend a specialist evaluation. This is important, because of a clause in my contract that my clients are required to initial by which they agree to hold me harmless from any subsequent action resulting from an alleged defect or deficiency involving any component I'd recommended for service, and why not? I'm a generalist not a specialist, or so my standards confirm.

Encouraged by my newfound expertise, I examined other components with equal care. Vent pipes have to be an approved type, perfectly sealed, adequately pitched, and have appropriate clearances from combustibles, return-air compartments had to contain the piercing beam of my military flashlight and be spotlessly clean, or risk being identified as a potential haven for dust mites and other contaminants that can compromise air quality. I want to be the first to warn my clients about environmental contaminants, and not the one who learns about it later from their attorneys when they've been diagnosed with so-called respiratory problems. Attorneys don't contact you to report that their clients have had sneezing fits caused by springtime allergies, dirty filters, or animal dander. Instead, they tell of family members afflicted by daily nosebleeds and blinding headaches, and who are gasping for breath at death's door. Then, after they receive an infusion of money from an insurance company, they make a miraculous recovery, list their house for sale, and move higher up the hill where the grass is greener and the air is cleaner. And it's not unusual for attorneys to find a host of expert witnesses willing to confirm such horror stories for a handful of silver.

So how can inspectors defend against such spurious claims? Well, if you believe that all attorneys are fair and reasonable and believe in justice, don't do anything and trust in the judicial system. However, if you believe that many attorneys make false accusations and resort to ridiculous exaggerations, then your reports should include information that reminds your clients that their health is their responsibility and not yours, and that they should have the air quality tested and distribution ducts cleaned as a prudent investment in health and environmental hygiene, and particularly if they or any member of their family suffer from allergies or asthma. After all, that's a perfectly reasonable recommendation and one that should appear in every report. Written words are a powerful means of defense, but let's talk about ducts.

The best ducts are relatively new, black or silver and flexible, and run in a straight line or curve gently, and all other types are suspect. Flexible ones with a blueish-gray sleeve are u-v susceptible and often look as if they've been slashed and shredded with a razor knife, compressed fiberglass ones can evoke allergic responses, and old rigid metal ones could be heat-only, or are insulated with a silver or milky-white corrugated sleeve that typically includes asbestos that should never be endorsed under any circumstances. Asbestos is a highly emotional and contentious issue. Even the innocent-looking milky-white paper seals on the seams of plenums and heat vents and around the boots of many old ducts, should be reported as being a suspected asbestos-containing-material that should be evaluated by a specialist, regardless of their condition. In addition, the ducts should be adequately supported, and their seams should be sealed with a silver thermal duct tape, and not the old gray duct tape that typically dries out and falls off. Regardless, you should take a photograph of the ducts to document their condition. Remember, even when you find perfect ducts, other inspectors or service personnel could come behind you and cause damage that you could never prove didn't exist at the time of your inspection. Remember, this is not about winning a lawsuit it's about avoiding one.

The most frightening aspect of fossil-fueled heating systems is their ability to produce carbon monoxide, a gas known as the silent-killer because it cannot be seen, smelled, or tasted. If you're not prepared to use a carbon monoxide tester, the use of which only confirms a condition at a given point in time, you should be prepared to confirm that any appliance capable of producing such a deadly gas is reasonably modern, perfectly clean, well sealed, directly vented, richly infused with combustion air, and has burner flames that are cobalt blue and stand straight up. If they're yellow and heavily oxygenated, and the tips bend over and dance after the blower fan turns on there's the likelihood of a cracked firebox, inadequate combustion air, or simply a maladjusted gas/oxygen ratio, any of which can contribute to the production of carbon monoxide. However, regardless of regional codes, I never endorsed any combustion appliance in sleeping quarters, even if it's directly vented. In addition, I'm suspicious of any appliance that's older than ten years, although combustion appliances in newer homes are also a concern, because newer homes are better insulated than older ones and more tightly sealed, and something as seemingly innocent as a bathroom exhaust fan can induce negative pressure and back-drafting.

Air-conditioning systems are more complicated than heating systems but not life-threatening, and I'll be the first to admit that for many years I didn't have a clue about how they worked, not that I'm an expert now. However, with the help of others and specialized instruments I can better evaluate their performance. The first thing I take into consideration is the size and age of the residence, and its orientation to the sun. This will tell me a lot about the thermal value of its walls and windows. Obviously, a two-story house with a southern exposure and single-glazed windows will be hard to cool, and particular if the blower fan is on the ground floor. We all know that hot air rises, and cold air falls and is sluggish and more difficult to move. The first time I was threatened with a lawsuit was over air-conditioning, was by a client who was a college professor and a person one might assume to be honorable but wasn't. In fact, he forced me to remind myself about a parable I'd been told as a child that was intended to instruct me the ways of the world. It went something like this. A frog was basking on a riverbank when it saw a scorpion approaching. Alarmed, it was about to leap to safety in the water when the scorpion spoke. "Hey, hold on, I just want to talk to you for a moment." Still poised to leap, the frog paused to listen. "I'd like to get to the other side of the river where the grass is greener," explained the scorpion, "and I was wondering if you'd be kind enough to give me a ride on your back?" "You must be out of your mind," the frog replied, "you're a scorpion, and you'd sting me!" "Of course I wouldn't," the scorpion protested, "because if I did you'd die and I'd drown." Persuaded by the scorpion's impeccable logic, the frog agreed. The scorpion scurried onto the frog's back, and they began the long journey across the river. Halfway across, the scorpion arched its tail over its body, and injected the frog with its fatal venom. "Oh, no," moaned the frog with its dying breath, "you said you wouldn't sting me." "I know I did," the scorpion agreed, "but I just couldn't help myself; it's in my nature." This parable is one that inspectors would do well to remember. I digress, but here's the story of the professor and his threatened lawsuit.

The house I inspected for him was an old two-story Spanish house with a balcony on the second floor with a southern exposure that had been enclosed with slatted windows, and which he planned to use as an office. Significantly, it was in the middle of winter when I did the inspection, but when he told me about its intended use I warned him that it would be uncomfortably hot on long summer days. This not only proved to be true, but also the reason why he was threatening to sue me. It was the middle of a sweltering summer when he called to complain, but he didn't have the courage to complain directly. Instead, he told me that he was divorced and that it was his visiting daughter who'd complained about the uncomfortably warm temperature on the second floor. However, I hadn't endorsed the system. My report indicated that it was relatively new, and advised him to obtain the installation permit and transferable warranty. However, I'd also recommended service because a stray cat was sheltering from the winter cold inside a separated duct in the foundation crawlspace. When I reminded him about this, he had a sudden lapse of memory but insisted that subsequent to his daughter's complaint a heating and air-conditioning contractor had recommended that the entire system be replaced, for a cost of fifteen thousand dollars. I was shocked, but then he told me that he didn't expect me to pay for it and, instead, he wanted me to turn-in a claim to my insurance company, who he reasoned would pay and after which he'd reimburse the cost of my deductible. I wanted to tell him to go straight to hell, but I didn't. I told him that I'd charitably give him the cost of my deductible and not a penny more to hold me harmless. "Take it or leave it," I told him. He took it. So what can be learned from this tale other than the fact that I paid to avoid a lawsuit and that professors can be as corrupt as common criminals?

I can't speak for other inspectors and I wouldn't want to if I could, but I'm convinced that most inspectors will eventually do highly sophisticated inspections with specialized instruments, and impart information in exquisitely detailed reports, replete with annotated pictures, for which they'll receive fees at least equal to those of structural engineers, geologists, and other specialists. Regardless, here's a tale about another system that I inspected that illustrates how a series of seemingly unrelated issues could embroil an inspector in a lawsuit. In today's sue-happy society, it's not enough to report that a system is working or not working, it needs to be described in detail.

I recently completed an inspection of a two-story house with a raised foundation and single-glazed windows, built in 1942. The heating and air conditioning were not original, but were beyond their design-life. The furnace and evaporator coil were on a return-air plenum sheathed with plywood in an exterior closet that was linked by ducts in the foundation crawlspace to two small side-by-side return-air grills in a hallway at the center of the house. The condensing coil was leaning on a pad that had settled out of level in an adjacent side yard. The system responded and, therefore, could be said to be working, and this is what the real estate agent wanted me to report. But, there were problems. The return-air plenum was not sealed and extremely dirty, and it had been subject to moisture contamination over the years because tree roots had raised a patio slab on which the furnace closet stood and caused water to drain toward it. In addition, the return-air compartment and most of the supply ducts that ran through the foundation crawlspace were "Air-Cell," or insulated with a known asbestos-containing-material. The ducts were definitely original and likely intended for a heat-only system, and therefore could be argued to be too small for cold air, which is sluggish and more difficult to move. Remember, the house is two-story, has single-glazed windows and walls that are not insulated, and the return-air grills and blower fan are on the ground floor. Add to these facts that the house is in southern California where the temperature regularly exceeds one-hundred degrees and, therefore, the air-conditioning system was suspect at best. To complicate matters, portions of the Air-Cell ducts had been replaced with portions of fiberglass Micro-Air ducts as well as more modern flexible ones. This could be alleged to be an improvement, but that would be a mistake because an attorney could argue that attaching new ducts to the original Air-Cell ducts allowed for the possibility that the air supply had been contaminated with a known carcinogen. That could be a difficult argument to prove, but when it comes to asbestos any defense is doomed to fail, as most attorneys and veteran inspectors know only too well.

As I contemplated how best to advise my client, I found myself faced with an interesting ethical question that I'd asked myself before. Am I a generalist, a specialist, or perhaps a humanist, in the ordinary sense of the word? I've written about how the distinction between generalists and specialists has become blurred over the years, and expressed the opinion that pleading "the generalist defense" is a total waste of time. And, remember, about ninety-nine percent of all lawsuits are settled before they get to court and the trick is to avoid being sued. Regardless, we know that a generalist is obligated to defer to a specialist. However, we also know that a specialist hired by the sellers is likely to merely correct the defects and leave it at that. And, therefore, the potential of a lawsuit would remain if all I did was to defer to a specialist. Regardless, I was not about to leave myself vulnerable to a complaint, let alone a lawsuit, and advised my clients as follows:

The system is not original, but beyond its design life and needs to be serviced. However, I would question the wisdom of spending money on a system that's old and inefficient and would not meet reasonable performance expectations. Regardless, a two-story house with single-glazed windows and walls that are not insulated would be better served by two systems. If this is not done and the windows are not exchanged for dual-glazed ones, you're not likely to be satisfied with the performance of the air-conditioning on the second floor during the summer months. As the system exists, various components need to be serviced: The condensing coil in the south side yard sits out of level, which will stress the fan-motor bearing; the flexible gas feed pipe on the furnace should be rigid until it passes beyond the casing; the return-air compartment and its ducts are old, dirty, and not adequately sealed, and portions of them in the exterior furnace cabinet have been contaminated by vermin. Also, the ducts that pass through the foundation crawlspace have been unprofessionally modified. For the most part, they consist of the original "Air-Cell" ducts that are insulated with a known asbestos-containing-material, portions of which have been replaced with "Micro-Air" fiberglass ducts and a more modern flexible one. Regardless, the original "Air-Cell" ducts were intended for heat-only and are too small for air-conditioning, but opening and replacing sections of them created the potential for asbestos contamination of the circulating air. In summary, although my responsibility is limited to recommending that an HVAC contractor and asbestos specialist evaluate the system, common sense compels me to recommend that you obtain estimates for replacing and upgrading the entire system.

Here's the moral to this story and remember truth is relative, but as far as the real estate agents were concerned I likely became a deal-killer that day. It really doesn't matter, and particularly whether you define yourself as a generalist or a specialist or simply someone blessed with the ability to reason, just don't leave yourself vulnerable to a lawsuit. If you know anything at all about real estate lawsuits, you'll know that those of us with insurance might as well walk around with large targets painted on our backs.

Pools and Spas

I enjoy evaluating in-ground pools and spas and typically charge an additional eighty-five to one-hundred dollars. Truth is relative, and so are my fees. Anyway, when it comes to pools and spas, I have a detailed disclaimer about leakage that prints automatically as follows:

Pools and spas occasionally leak, but without specialized equipment this may be impossible to confirm. However, it could become apparent from secondary evidence during our inspection, which is purely visual. Regardless, the owner or the occupant of a property would be aware that the water level drops regularly and must be topped off, and this should be disclosed. Unusually high water bills could reveal this, but only a pressure test of the pipes, a dye test of cracks, or a geo-phone test of specific areas would confirm it, and any such specialized tests are beyond the scope of our service.

Therefore, you should ask the sellers to guarantee that the pool/spa does not leak, request to review the water bills for a twelve-month period, or obtain comprehensive insurance to cover such an eventuality.

A few years ago, I inspected a unique pool/spa. The pool was not much wider than a garage, and it and spa were installed with permit over a structural concrete vault above a five car garage. I didn't measure the height of the vault, but it was completely accessible and could be entered through a hatch in the corner of a fourteen-foot garage ceiling, which eventually allowed me to confirm that moisture and minerals were leeching through a side wall of the spa, but that's not what concerned me. What concerned me was sensible access and egress to and from the pool. From this point, I'll just say "access," instead of repeating "access and egress." But, study the following photographs, and notice a clear view of the street below in the first picture and the rooftops in the second. I avoid including myself in pictures for reports, but that's me shown furthest away in the second picture on the next page.

Access at the deep-end is impossible and prevented by a guardrail that separates the pool from an adjacent guest bedroom deck, shown in the first picture. Access from a deck at the shallow end appears to be adequate but it's not; look closely. A spa takes up most of the deck area, which leaves only the narrow step-access with no handrail. I suppose one could enter the pool by stepping down into the spa and climbing over the spillway, or by foolishly stepping onto the architectural capstone at the edge of the spa, but that would be foolish. Besides, it's loose, cracked in half, and dangerous. This leaves the sides. Look closely at both, and notice particularly the huge drop to the street below.

As you can see, there are French doors on the house that open onto a sixteen-inch strip of coping stone, meaning that one could access the pool by simply opening a French door and stepping out and jumping in. Naturally, one could risk injury by jumping in but, given the width of the pool, diving in would be dangerous. However, both are reasonable alternatives when one considers the last option, which is to enter the pool in the same way from the far side. As you can clearly see, there's a narrow strip of coping stone that's only slightly wider than that outside the French doors and, therefore, perhaps more inviting, but it's paralleled by a short guardrail and the only barrier between the pool and what must be at least a twenty foot drop to the street below. I didn't actually take measurements, including guardrail or the drop to the street, but compare the height of the guardrail by the pool to the height of that where I'm standing with others.

Whoever designed this pool, whoever built it, and whoever approved the permit and then issued a Certificate of Occupancy, confirms why Los Angeles is known as La-la-land, and that's why simply disclaiming a code-compliance inspection, or relying on permits as

65

a means of defense, is an absolute waste of time. Not only is this pool/spa an insult to common sense, it's a lawsuit waiting to happen. And, remember, built to code means built to the lowest possible standard, and a permit is nothing more than a piece of paper issued by a bureaucrat who's indemnified against prosecution. But here's the rub. As a California inspector, I was tied to this abomination for four long years, and there's absolutely no doubt in my mind that death or serious injury is just a foolish act away by a guest, a conscientious gardener attending to the plants, an adolescent, or even another inspector silly enough to take a walk on the wrong side of this pool. Furthermore, every attorney in California knows that decent inspectors carry insurance, which is tantamount to inspectors walking around with bullhorns, announcing they have insurance and inviting their clients to sue them. To make matters worse, the mindless equitable indemnity law in California will continue to ensure that inspectors will be dragged into endless lawsuits, in which huge sums of money will find its way into the pockets of unscrupulous clients and their attorneys, and that's just the way it is in La-la-land. [The statute of limitations on this pool has passed, but I submitted the article and its pictures for publication solely as a means of defense because, even though my evaluation of the pool/spa left no doubt that I regarded it as safety-hazard and an insult to intelligence, I still felt vulnerable to a lawsuit].

Environmental Contaminants

When most inspectors think of environmental contaminants, they probably think of asbestos. Once hailed as the "miracle fiber," it has been in use throughout recorded history. It was treasured by the ancient Greeks and Romans and woven into tablecloths that were cleaned by being tossed into a fire, and it was also woven into wicks for the lamps that lit their sacred places. In the modern world however, asbestos struck fear into the public psyche, and generated thousands of lawsuits. Most involved its presence in siding and roofing material, common household plaster, drywall mud, acoustical ceilings, and duct insulation, and few if any defendants managed to prevail. Rational defenses were powerless. It didn't seem to matter that the US Consumer Product Safety Commission and also the Environmental Protection Agency advised homeowners that: "In most cases, asbestos containing materials are best left alone." And, it didn't seem to matter that the asbestos in common residential usage was almost exclusively a long fiber type of the white serpentine group, called Chrysotile, which was unlikely to find its way into the alveoli of the lungs where it could metastasize. But, once the word "asbestos" was uttered it reverberated throughout the courts of the land and created a metaphoric gold-rush in the inspection industry, in which thousands of attorneys struck pay dirt. For this reason, my reports not only inform my clients about asbestos but also about its potential sources, if the age of a house happens to warrant it. Here's an example of a general narrative that prints automatically in my reports:

Most homes built after 1978, are generally assumed to be free of asbestos and many other common environmental contaminants. However, as a courtesy to our clients, we are including some well documented, and therefore public, information about several environmental contaminants that could be of concern to you and your family, all of which we do not have the expertise or the authority to evaluate, such as asbestos, radon, methane, formaldehyde, termites and other wood-destroying organisms, pests and rodents, molds, microbes, bacterial organisms, and electromagnetic radiation, to name some of the more commonplace ones. Nevertheless, we will attempt to alert you to any suspicious substances that would warrant evaluation by a specialist. However, health and safety and environmental hygiene are deeply personal responsibilities, and you should make sure that you are familiar with any contaminant that could affect your family and your home environment. You can learn more about contaminants from a booklet published by The Environmental Protection Agency, which you can read online at www.epa.gov/iaq/pubs

I have other narratives that I can select, involving a laundry list of other contaminants that I include in almost every report. Not too long ago, I used to believe that consumers were responsible for educating themselves about such things, and certainly responsible for their own health, but when there's easy money to be made they can become as helpless as children and collapse weeping into the arms of their expensive attorneys. However, I'm happy to report that the threat of asbestos seems to have run its course. However, I'm sorry to report that the threat of asbestos has been replaced by the threat of mold that appears to be popping up like mushrooms, or would it be more appropriate to say truffles, which are a very expensive fungi affordable only to the wealthy?

I intend to report on yet another outrageous mold case when I have all the facts, but it's too late for this book. However, I'm not an authority on molds and fungi and will not make statements that I cannot document. Although much has been written about molds, the specific mechanism of the disease and its effects on human health are not yet fully understood and professional opinions are not uniform. This much is sure however, mold has been around since the beginning of recorded time and is essential to the life process. It must have cellulose material and a water source to survive, and it's usually visible or discernible by a musty or moldy odor, which should not be confused with the acrid smell of rodent urine or the bacterial odor of decay from decomposing carcasses. Not all molds are a health-threat, but at this time mold seems to be manna from heaven for some attorneys, who are invigorated by the smell of money. Interestingly, I've been told by persons who should know that mold will not result in the hundreds and hundreds of lawsuits that have been generated by asbestos, but I'm certainly not convinced. Reasoning from the limited evidence at hand, I believe we'll be seeing more and more mold lawsuits. If I'm right, this is bad news indeed for inspectors nationwide and we should continue to do everything we can to avoid a mold lawsuit. Regardless, here's what I have to say about mold which prints automatically in my reports:

Mold is a microorganism that has tiny seeds, or spores, that are spread on the air, land, and feed on organic matter. It has been in existence throughout human history, and actually contributes to the life process. It takes many different forms, many of them benign, like mildew. Some characterized as allergens are relatively benign but can provoke allergic reactions among sensitive people, and others characterized as pathogens can have adverse health effects on large segments of the population, such as the very young, the elderly, and people with suppressed immune systems. However, there are less common molds that are called toxigens that represent a serious health threat. All molds flourish in the presence of moisture, and we make a concerted effort to look for any evidence of it wherever there could be a water source, including that from condensation. Interestingly, the molds that commonly appear on the grout joints of ceramic tiles in bathrooms do not usually constitute a health threat, but they should be removed. However, some visibly similar molds that form on cellulose materials, such as on drywall, plaster, and wood, are potentially toxigenic. If mold is to be found anywhere within a home, it will likely be in the area of tubs, showers, toilets, sinks, water heaters, evaporator coils, inside attics with bathroom exhaust fans that are not ducted to the exterior, and return-air compartments that draw outside air, which we do not endorse. Nevertheless, mold can appear as though spontaneously at any time, so you should be prepared to monitor your home, and particularly those areas that we identified. Naturally, it's equally important to maintain clean air-supply ducts and to change filters frequently, because contaminated ducts are a common breeding ground for dust mites and other contaminants. Regardless, the specific identification of molds can only be determined by specialists and laboratory analysis, and is absolutely beyond the scope of our inspection. Nonetheless, as a prudent investment in environmental hygiene, we recommend that you have your home tested for the presence of any such contaminants, and particularly if you or any member of your family suffers from allergies or asthma. Also, you can learn more about mold online from the "Environmental Protection Agency."

In addition to this, I also have a disclaimer in a new section of my report-writer called "Health & Safety," which I hope provides me with even greater protection. Remember, it doesn't hurt to repeat something in order to make a point. I bet many of us can still hear the stern voice of a parent echoing down through the years. I know I can still hear a teacher's rhetorical question echoing from the distant stone corridors of my school: "Master Swift, how many times do you have to be told not to run in the corridors?" (Students in my boarding school had titles, hence "master"). To this day, I never run in corridors crowded with people. Anyway, here's the other mold narrative I mentioned:

We do not test for mold or measure indoor air quality, which the Consumer Product Safety Commission ranks fifth among potential contaminants. Regardless, a person's health is a truly personal responsibility, and inasmuch as we not inspect for mold or test for other environmental contaminants we recommend that you schedule an inspection by an environmental hygienist before the close of escrow. And this would be imperative if you or any member of your family suffers from allergies or asthma, and could require the sanitizing of air ducts and other concealed areas. Mold cannot exist without moisture. Therefore, any moisture, whether it be from inadequate grading and drainage, a leaking roof, window, or door, or moisture from a faulty exhaust vent, a condensate pipe, an evaporator coil, or a component of a plumbing system should be serviced immediately, or the potential for mold contamination will remain.

I even have a group of narratives from which I can select when I find evidence of a plumbing leak or moisture intrusion that warns about the potential for mold. I even have one that reports on a "mold-like" substance and recommends service, but I won't bore you with more examples, but let me warn you that mold lawsuits pose a threat that's not likely to go away any time soon. However, help yourself to all or any part of these narratives that you might need. And hope and pray for justice, but don't count on it. Meanwhile, here's an article that I wrote about my own experience with mold, which I promised to tell you about earlier, which I called: "A Case for Common Sense."

Some years ago now, I went to my mailbox and found a box of homemade cake and cookies from a gracious client and, also, a summons from an attorney. The cake and cookies were a complete surprise, the summons was not; that's how crazy things are in Los Angeles, and probably why it's known as La-la-land. I consoled myself with a cookie, and went home to read the summons and review my report. The summons relates that after a weekend of continuous rain the plaintiffs noticed that an edge of carpet in their condominium was damp. They notified the home owners' association, who immediately agreed to correct what was apparently part of a problem with grading and drainage that they were literally in the process of correcting. However, after weeks of indecision and delay, and with work underway in the in the middle of the rainy season, during which time walls were opened and left open, the plaintiffs suddenly began to suffer headaches, respiratory ailments, and an emotional angst that no doubt inspired them to call an attorney who immediately filed suit against a whole tribe of people.

"What has this to do with me?" I asked myself. On a condominium inspection I not only disclaim an evaluation of everything beyond the unit but I particularly disclaim grading and drainage, which is the responsibility of the home owners' association. Nonetheless, I read on and realized that I'd not been informed about the problem, which is a violation of my contract. And I also learned that there was no evidence of moisture intrusion when I inspected the unit and, furthermore, I confirmed that the people suing me weren't my clients. My clients had cancelled escrow several months before these enterprising plaintiffs purchased the unit. They'd simply obtained a copy of my report without paying for it and felt that they were entitled to sue me, probably on the blatantly immoral advice of their attorney. But, does that make them any less responsible for their actions? Regardless, what does that tell us about the value of our contracts, our standards, our common sense, and about truth itself?

If this had happened to you instead of me, wouldn't you shake your head in disgust? As for me, I felt similar to the way I felt on 9/11: angry, disgusted, vengeful, and powerless to do anything about it. I turned the case over to my insurance company and it was settled. But let's forget about the lawsuit, and talk about principles of right, and wrong, and commonsense principles that are essential to the education of every child and which underpin civilized society and the very foundation of our judicial system. Much of what I'm going to say I've said before, but it's worth repeating. In the first few pages of this book I quoted from Bill O'Reilly's, Who's Looking Out for You, in which he states that our civil justice system has become "a cesspool of corruption" (p.166), and although I'm not an admirer of O'Reilly I have a doctoral degree in English and can assure you that the "cesspool" metaphor is an intentionally dramatic and legitimate use of ironic over-statement and that the logic of his argument is beyond dispute: He tells the truth and supports it with proof, which is more than I can say about many of the legal briefs that I've read over the years. I will admit that a fellow inspector once described my articles as 'tirades," and I can understand that because I have no tolerance for injustice and those who prey on the innocent. However, I've never met an inspector who disagreed with me, let alone an attorney who was able to refute my arguments—not one, not ever. True, many well-meaning inspectors and one attorney advised me not to take legal issues so seriously, and to simply accept them as a necessary evil that we have to live with, but I'll never do that. Justice is worth fighting for, and I'll never countenance evil in whatever forms it takes.

Like me, most of you probably have a disclaimer in your reports that confirms that it's non-transferable. Isn't that common sense? After all, we wouldn't want every Tom, Dick, and Harry to be able to access our reports without paying for them, and then be able to use them against us in a lawsuit. However, every Tom, Dick, and Harry can do that in California, thanks to one shortsighted attorney and an insane case law. Not only are we responsible for the properties that we inspect for four years, but anyone that obtains our reports is legally entitled to sue us whether they pay for our service or not. The case law that allows this is comparable to the three-strikes-and-you're-out law, which seems reasonable in theory until we realize that a hungry felon could spend the rest of his life in prison for stealing a loaf of bread. That's not right, that's bloody barbaric and flies in the face of common sense. But that's exactly the plight of inspectors in California, and probably in many other states as well, who remain the potential victims of every unscrupulous plaintiff and attorney who abuses the law in blatant disregard of truth and justice. I've said this before, and I'll say it again: our contracts and standards were written by the best minds in the business, but some attorneys treat them like toilet paper. Frivolous lawsuits are epidemic in our industry, and sooner or later we're going to have to unite with the real estate industry and do something about it.

Wood Destroying Organisms, Pests and Rodents

Industry standards and many inspection contracts commonly disclaim an inspection for termites, dry rot, mold or fungi, wood destroying organisms, and pests and rodents, which are generally considered to be the responsibility of state-licensed termite inspectors. However, fearing lawsuits, many inspectors now document such damage in their reports, including damage by pests and rodents. Rats, mice, and even common household pets, can damage components that inspectors are responsible for evaluating, and which can have an adverse effect on health. For instance, inspectors frequently find supply ducts that have been gnawed and contaminated by animal waste and some that are actually inhabited by vermin. However, they should decide in advance what they're willing to accept responsibility for and what risks they're willing to assume. They're completely within their rights to disclaim something, but it should be clearly documented within a contract or service description, and I favor restating a disclaimer within the body of the report. For instance, I commonly use this narrative:

Vermin and other pests are part of the natural habitat, but they often invade homes. Rats and mice have collapsible rib-cages and can enter even the tiniest crevices. And it is not uncommon for them to establish colonies in crawlspaces, attics, closets, and even inside walls, where they can breed unseen and become a health threat. Therefore, it would be prudent to make sure that a home is rodent-proof, and to monitor those areas that are not readily visible.

Rest assured that I have many similar narratives stored in my report-writer, which I regard as ammunition, and believe me when I tell you that if I see as much as one rat dropping I recommend an evaluation by an exterminator. You may think that this is overkill, but I remind myself of an old Chinese aphorism, "one rat turd ruins the rice," and ask me to tell you about some of the lawsuits I've read involving rats, mice, and other vermin, because they'll make you a believer. Also, you should be aware that rodent teeth continue to grow throughout their lifetime, and they must gnaw on things to sharpen them, and I've actually documented my reports with pictures of Romex sheathing gnawed by rodents. Regardless, let's continue with a story about a fungus that has become infamous and described as "the house cancer." It's called Poria Incrassata, and it can appear as though spontaneously and destroy cellulose materials in a matter of weeks.

Before telling you about Poria, let me repeat that the best articles I've read about mold and its effects on health and the environment are by Dr. Ronald E. Gots, who I mentioned earlier in a discussion of grading and drainage. His articles are truly worth reading, but not everyone agrees with him. Regardless, I became particularly interested in Poria when I learned about it and then witnessed its awesome power. It's not mold, and because it's dependent on moisture from the soil and not from a plumbing leak you're not likely to see it within the living space, although it could appear as dust-like spores, dark stains, or shrunken wood, but you can be sure that there's more credible evidence of it concealed elsewhere. For instance, you might discover mushroom-like fruiting bodies or delicate fan-like fronds that are called rhizomorphs spreading over the soil and on surfaces that could well be in the advanced stages of decay and structural failure.

The worst case of Poria Incrassata that I heard about began innocently enough. Escrow had closed on an expensive two-story house, and a painter was finishing the inside of a kitchen cabinet when his brush literally broke a surface. After further probing, it was decided that the upper cabinets and then the lower cabinets and counters had to be removed to expose a greater area. The new owners hadn't moved in but were opposed to it and then agreed, but it didn't end there. Eventually, an entire wall was opened up and revealed the dank remains of studs that looked like shrunken mummified skin, but which were all that were left supporting a section of floor joists in a bedroom above. This explained why the bedroom floor sloped but no one, not even an inspector, questioned it. But, to jump to the end of the story, the owners never moved into their dream home, and a lawsuit ensued with claims that far exceeded the sale's price of the house. Would a first-rate inspector have discovered this? It's possible, because the sloping bedroom floor was certainly evidence of a structural anomaly in a given area, which ruled out general differential settling and which should have been recommended for a specialist evaluation.

I became so fascinated by Poria's awesome power that I arranged a weekend buffet lunch at my home, invited a few local inspectors, and paid one of the two most foremost experts in the country to give a slide-presentation and teach us as much as he could. Therefore, it would not be inaccurate for me to say that I learned from the best. However, I never would have guessed that I would later be drawn into a lawsuit over the infamous Poria. The case in which I was involved also began innocently enough. During my inspection of a foundation crawlspace, I noticed that a section of cripple wall had been replaced, and deduced that the original one had rotted out, probably because parts of it had been below the exterior grade. The quality of the repair work was poor, the studs were not sixteen inches on center, the nail pattern was sloppy, and shear paneling had not been added, as it should have been to meet the current seismic standards, all of which I noted in my report. However, without going into details, and because the work was relatively new and the negative grading had been corrected, I was content to describe what I'd seen and recommend that my clients obtain the necessary documentation to confirm that the work was done with permit by a professional, and to have the cripple walls upgraded to include shear paneling.

Several months later, my clients called to tell me about a dust-like substance adjacent to a baseboard in their bedroom they'd wiped away but had reappeared. I offered to look at it before my inspection on the following morning, which I did. As soon as I saw it, it looked like spores from a fruiting body, but I put on my coveralls, crawled into the foundation space, and was greeted by the view of the Poria that you see in the long-shot and close-up pictures shown on the next page. As a point if interest, notice the new framing that I mentioned and the absence of shear-paneling on the cripple-walls that I'd recommended be installed.

Even knowing how aggressive Poria is, it was hard for me to believe how quickly it had appeared and spread, and if you don't know about Poria you may find it hard to believe. However, the cripple walls were pristine just a few months before, and I could prove it. In fact, as you can see, portions of the wood still look new. However, a termite report that was performed weeks after my inspection found what was identified as a common fungus and treated it locally. Of course, although I recognized what I was now seeing, I advised my clients to call the termite company immediately, because state law actually prohibited me from commenting on damage from termites or any other wood-destroying organism.

My clients were expecting their first baby, and were naturally concerned about their health and that of their unborn child, but I assured them that Poria is not a health-hazard, and gave them the name of the same expert who'd educated me years earlier. They were relieved and thanked me, and I left feeling like a Good Samaritan. A few weeks later, they sued me, the sellers, the termite inspector, both real estate agents, and a host of others for all I know. As I mentioned earlier, their attorney failed to get my name right, misrepresented me as the owner of a termite company, and related a long and overstated account of the pain and suffering and emotional distress that my alleged negligence had caused the expectant couple. However, besides the factual errors, it failed to mention the indisputable truth that I was the first person to come to their aid and the one who'd given them the name and telephone number of the preeminent Poria specialist. It goes without saying that their attorney must have asked them how they became aware of the Poria in the first place, and yet this materially significant fact was conveniently omitted. "Why would they do this to me," I wondered? "What could make a pleasant young couple become so suddenly wicked? Was it the lure of easy money, or was it on the insistence of a sleazy attorney?" By way of interest, their attorney tried to recruit the same Poria authority who'd taught me as an expert witness, but the expert refused unless they agreed to drop the charges against me, but they were looking for every penny they could get. Besides being the foremost expert on Poria, he also happens to be a termite inspector and an honorable man indeed. His name is Luis de la Cruz. There were other mitigating facts that you'd find amazing, but it's not important now. I guess even truth itself becomes immaterial sometimes.

He was deposed as an expert witness, and the case dragged while the costs mounted on both sides. My insurance company settled, and my name was added to the growing list of innocent inspectors who've been victimized. Please don't ask me what happens to the truth in lawsuits. Ordinary people become wicked, and some attorneys don't seem to give a damn about truth or the facts of a case. A fellow inspector said that I shouldn't have returned to the property, but that wouldn't have changed anything. Besides, should we train ourselves to deny the human impulse to help one other? I still feel good about what I did. However, the experience certainly changed the way I now report on things. Since that time, if I see any framing repairs anywhere, I not only recommend that my clients obtain the necessary permits but that they ascertain what occasioned the repairs, and after which I disclaim any further responsibility regardless of the quality of the work and recommend that they seek a second opinion from a specialist. Isn't it a shame to be forced to such extremes?

CHAPTER FIVE

Marketing

I've never thought much about marketing, because I started doing inspections in a golden age when realtors were scrambling for home inspectors. Consequently, I acquired a large following and never had to look for work again, although most of my bookings came from truly professional realtors or client referrals. In fact, I regularly declined about fifteen inspections a week, and for a while I referred many clients to an inspector who later agreed to be an expert witness against me but denied it to my face. The case never went to court, but if it had he would have been exposed for the falling-down drunk that he is. Since then, I've steadily increased my fees and limited myself to one leisurely inspection a day. I'd rather do one inspection a day for six or seven hundred that two for three-fifty. Besides, being sued is a numbers game. However, I like to keep my finger on the pulse of the home inspection business, and did write a brief marketing article entitled "Image Is," after being aggravated by a so-called documentary about home inspections on national television. This is what I wrote.

Image is everything, or so it has been said, and it can influence an opinion of people and services. So I was particularly concerned by the spectacle of incompetent inspectors being paraded on primetime television for everyone to see. Of course, the content was more entertaining than educational, but it certainly tarnished the image of inspectors. I've mentioned this in other articles, and suggested that we need to do something about improving our image. I've also pointed out that although real estate agents are statistically ranked on a par with used car salesmen they still view themselves as professionals who're entitled to a commission relative to the sale's price of a house. Interestingly, many of them tacitly confirm how little they value the service of inspectors by shopping for cheap ones who base their fees solely on the square foot size of a house and not on its value, and yet don't bat an eyelid when geologists and structural engineers demand significantly higher fees for their services. It doesn't make any sense, but then sometimes the truth really is stranger than fiction.

I'm reminded of something that a veteran inspector had to say in his retirement speech at a conference in Oregon. He was concerned about the welfare of inspectors following in his footsteps and about the future of the industry in general, and had this to say. I don't remember exactly what he said but it went something like this: "Knowing that I was going to retire in a year, I raised my prices, and started to get more work than I could handle. So, I raised my prices again and got even more work. So, I raised my prices yet again." He went on to explain that he couldn't understand why this had happened, but assured everyone that indeed it had and made him wish that he'd raised his prices years earlier. However, hearing that he had been a truly conscientious inspector and believing that most people realize they get what they pay for, I could understand it. And whereas I also believe that everyone has the right to make a living as best they can, I don't believe that inspectors who demean the image of their profession by performing multiple cheap inspections every day deserve the respect of their peers. And, please, don't accuse me of being an advocate of price-fixing. I'm an advocate of common sense and justice. Medical doctors and chiropractors share the title of "doctor," and yet the extent of their medical knowledge and the value of their expertise are in no way comparable. This is equally true of inspectors, and to repeat an ancient Chinese axiom: "One rat turd ruins the rice."

The main reason that the issue of price and image is particularly important to inspectors is because twenty-five percent of us are going to be sued and our insurance carriers are going to roll-over rather than defend us, as I've been repeating to the point of tedium throughout this book. Each and every day, inspectors become targets for unscrupulous clients and their attorneys simply because they have deep-pockets. Lawsuits are being settled for economic reasons, innocent inspectors are being denied an honorable defense, premiums are being raised, policies are being cancelled, and livelihoods are being jeopardized, and that's both a threat to our profession and a national disgrace. And it's very likely to get worse. Interestingly, some inspectors are actually cancelling their insurance policies and are prepared to hire their own attorney to defend them, and for that I salute them. The very best thing that inspectors could do for themselves now would be to raise their prices, put aside a percentage of each inspection for a defense fund, hope they never have to use it, conduct exemplary inspections, and represent themselves as the professionals they are, and who willingly accept the grave responsibilities of inspecting properties that far exceed those of real estate agents, structural engineers, and geologists combined.

POSTSCRIPT

Litigation is unpleasant, and when it's frivolous or unjust it can bring out the beast in even the most civilized person. So, let me put my experience as a building inspector into a larger and more positive context. I have no allegiance to any group, and as I said at the beginning it was never my intension to become a building inspector. I wanted to be a college professor and immerse myself in the classics, in the best that has been said and thought, but as fate and social circumstances would have it that was not to be. However, I have no regrets. Being an inspector allowed me to associate with a group of people who are "the salt of the earth," and I've still been able to follow my literary interests. I've also been fortunate enough to have made a lot of money, more than what I would have done as a tenured professor. And, although I've never counted the number of inspections I've done they number in the thousands, and in all the time they took I set and sailed my own course through the years, and was only occasionally assailed by the rough seas of circumstance and the barbarous attack of pirates. Regardless, for those of you who are just starting out, I wish you well, fair weather, and wind in your sails. Lastly, if you have any questions, or you just want to chat about the industry, you may call me. I'm in the Pacific Standard Time zone, and can be reached at (208) 916-8263.

www.ingramcontent.com/pod-product-compliance
Lightning Source LLC
Chambersburg PA
CBHW041450210326
41599CB00004B/202